The Day *JESUS* Did Tikkun Olam

(Repaired the World)

One often forgets that nothing in the New Testament is devoid of influence by the Jewish scriptures and rabbinic thought. *The Day Jesus Did Tikkun Olam* is an easy-to-read yet deeply scholarly study in which Dr. Rich Robinson explores ancient Jewish literature and lore to challenge the reader to think outside of the everyday Jewish box. Weaving together both Jewish and Christian scriptures, using relevant stories and citing biblical parallels, Robinson explains that the most significant Jewish value of *tikkun olam*—making this world a better place—is not only central to both religions, but central to the person of Jesus himself. The bridge is made and it's a fun bridge to cross. *The Day Jesus Did Tikkun Olam* is an important book for all who desire to understand the intimate connection between two great faiths, Judaism and Christianity.

—Murray Tilles, Director, Light of Messiah Ministries, M.Div, M.A. Counseling/Psychology, Trinity Evangelical Divinity School

This book is a treasure! Rich Robinson does us all a *mitzvah* [or 'favour' if you prefer] by telling us with his warmth, wit and sharp observations what it means to do *Tikkun Olam*—and how Jesus did this for us all. He brings a wealth of scholarship and contemporary relevance to the topic with great insights into Jewish ethics and the teachings of Jesus. Read and enjoy!

—Dr. Richard Harvey, Senior Researcher, Jews for Jesus

The Day Jesus Did Tikkun Olam is a joyful (re-)discovery of the Jesus who would be completely at home in our cousin club gatherings, needing absolutely no explanation why that "bagel" doesn't have a hole. Whatever you think about Jesus and the New Testament before you read this book, Dr. Robinson's witty and insightful book will put to rest any of your doubts about the Jewishness of Jesus and the message of the New Testament.

—Seth D. Postell, Academic Dean of Israel College of the Bible

Having been a Jewish believer in Jesus and a pastor for over 38 years, let me say that this book is a veritable goldmine of insights into the Jewishness of the New Testament. Writing in an engaging and accessible style, Robinson shows that Jesus stood firmly within biblical and post-biblical Jewish traditions. But he goes on to show that Jesus went beyond those traditions when he performed the ultimate act of "tikkun olam"—laying down his life to repair this sin-laden world. Read this book today and learn!

—Lon Solomon, Senior Pastor Emeritus, McLean Bible Church
Founder and President, Lon Solomon Ministries

It is a delight to endorse Rich Robinson's book *The Day Jesus Did Tikkun Olam.* As would be expected, he is a master at using humor to make difficult points or to go into territory that is rarely breached by the contemporary culture. But humor it the gift from Ha-Shem. It helps open the way that in ordinary circumstances would have been closed. It will be a treat for all who indulge themselves in this wonderful, but unusual monograph.

—Walter C. Kaiser, Jr.

Rich Robinson's study of the Jewish value of tikkun olam is enlightening, encouraging and very applicable to many of our recent struggles in contemporary society. The reader will gain some fresh insights on the Torah and the original Jewish context of Yeshua's teachings"

—Rabbi Barney Kasdan, Kehilat Ariel Messianic Synagogue, San Diego

The Day *JESUS* Did Tikkun Olam

(Repaired the World)

Jewish Values and the New Testament

RICHARD A. ROBINSON, Ph.D.

Lederer Books
An imprint of
Messianic Jewish Publishers
Clarksville, MD 21029

Printed in the United States of America

Cover design by Lisa Rubin,
Messianic Jewish Publishers
Graphic Design by Yvonne Vermillion,
Magic Graphix, Westfork, Arkansas

2018 1

ISBN 978-1-936716-98-2

Library of Congress Control Number: 2018958194

Published by:
Lederer Books
A Division of Messianic Jewish Publishers & Resources
6120 Day Long Lane
Clarksville, MD 21029

Distributed by:
Messianic Jewish Publishers & Resources
Order line: (800) 410-7367
lederer@messianicjewish.net
www.MessianicJewish.net

Table of Contents

FOREWORD

Readers interested in learning about Jesus' teachings, as well as Jewish and Christian ideas and ethics, will welcome Rich Robinson's new book *The Day Jesus Did Tikkun Olam*. This rich and learned book provides fresh insights into the messages of Jesus, by discussing their relation to Jewish wisdom of the Late Second Temple period and to the social teachings of the *Mishna.*

Robinson's original presentation follows a line of inquiry that is still relatively new among scholars writing about Jesus, early Christianity, and the Jewish rabbinical tradition. Since the Middle Ages, the common wisdom of both Christians and Jews had been that their respective religions were alien to each other theologically and carried different moral instructions.

The observation that Christianity and Judaism were actually sister religions, emerging from the same cradle, and with close systems of social ethics has been revolutionary. It came up for the first time in nineteenth-century Germany with the rise of a Jewish academic school of historical studies. Abraham Geiger and his disciples had pointed to huge similarities between Jesus' teachings and those of Mishnaic scholars of his time. Jesus, they claimed, preached messages that were similar to those of other Jewish groups and thinkers of the time, including the Pharisees and the *Hasidim*, an avant-garde group, whose teachings, some of them claimed, closely resembled those of Jesus and his circle.

In the 19th century and early 20th century, few were willing to give credence to what they saw as outlooks that blurred the differences between Judaism and Christianity. It was important for Christian and Jewish self-definition, as communities distant from each other, to look at Jesus' moral teachings as unique, not connected with the Judaism of his era.

The post-World War II years marked new attitudes on the part of many Christian and Jewish scholars towards the roots of Christianity. Following a hostile era in popular Christian attitudes toward Judaism and Jews in the pre WWII era, in the aftermath of the war, relationships began to change. Christian and Jewish thinkers came to acknowledge similarities between the two traditions. Scholarship stood on their side.

The discovery of the Dead Sea scrolls, in 1948, opened a new page in the study of Second Temple Judaism and early Christianity. David Flusser, a professor at the Hebrew University of Jerusalem, emerged as a leading scholar of the Dead Sea texts in light of Jesus' teachings and early Christian writings. He, and the Southern Baptist minister and scholar Robert Lindsey, established the Jerusalem School of Synoptic Research. Examining chapters and verses in Jewish and Christian texts from the first century of the Common Era, members of the small group pointed to striking similarities between Jesus' original sayings and those of the early masters of the Oral Law.

In recent years, researchers, including Amy-Jill Levine and Daniel Boyarin, have concluded that the dividing lines between the Christian and Jewish religious communities remained blurred for long generations with borderline groups that had not seeing contradiction between their Christian and Jewish affiliations operating in a number of geographical and cultural quarters. Such groups have come about again in the late modern era, promoting Jewish culture and identity coupled with faith in Jesus.

This excellent book gives evidence to this trend. Rich Robinson, the author, a Jewish believer in Jesus and a veteran scholar, has published numerous books and articles about Christian Jews, their history, faith and customs. Robinson, quite admirably, is in possession of remarkable knowledge about both Judaism and Christianity, as well as the communities and traditions that have come about in the borderlines between the two faiths. In *The Day Jesus did Tikkun Olam*, he utilizes his outstanding expertise on rabbinical Judaism, the New Testament and early Christianity, coupled with first hand familiarity with contemporary American culture, and a dynamic style, full of humor and wit. This makes for an enjoyable book, which comes as a bonus on top of the highly instructive value of the manuscript.

Yaakov Ariel
Professor of Religious Studies
The University of North Carolina at Chapel Hill

A Word About Names

Not everyone is familiar with the various Bible characters mentioned in this book. For that matter, not everyone is necessarily acquainted with the Bible itself. To serve as a brief orientation, here is a guide to some names and concepts you will encounter in these pages. Some of these terms are also collected in the glossary at the end.

The *Hebrew Bible*—also known as the *Tanakh*, the Old Testament, the First Testament, the Jewish Bible, etc.—depicts events from the creation of the world to about 400 B.C.E. *Tanakh* is an acronym for *T*orah, *N*evi'im, and *K*etuvim—the five books of Moses, the Prophets, and the Writings, the three sections of the Hebrew Bible.

The *New Testament*—some prefer Second Testament—depicts events taking place in the first decades of the first century C.E.

The *Torah* is the first five books of the Hebrew Bible: Genesis, Exodus, Leviticus, Numbers and Deuteronomy. The Torah is also known as the Five Books of Moses. In English, the Torah is sometimes called the Pentateuch, Greek for "five scrolls"—although today, the Torah is written on one scroll.

Moses is the central character in the early history of Israel.

The *prophets* were social guardians, bringing God's messages to the people. Frequently these were messages of warning in the face of societal wrongdoing, coupled with messages of hope for the future. Isaiah, Jeremiah and Ezekiel are the three "major" prophets, so called because their books are the longest among the prophets. "Minor," or shorter, prophets include Amos, Joel and Hosea.

The *gospels* are accounts of the life of Jesus. The word *gospel* means "good news." There are four gospels in the New Testament: Matthew, Mark, Luke and John. Each writer writes from his own perspective to highlight features of Jesus' life. Matthew, Mark and Luke often draw from the same source material and have similar accounts with minor variations. John stands apart from the other three stylistically and in content.

A *disciple* was a follower of Jesus (or of any teacher or rabbi, each of whom had their own disciples). An *apostle* was one of the twelve disciples specially selected by Jesus to work closely with him and learn from him. The *gospel* (singular) often refers to the message about Jesus as proclaimed by his followers, as distinguished from the four *gospels* (plural).

Acts is the New Testament book that tells about the early days of the Jesus movement, from the time when it was exclusively Jewish, then moving to embracing non-Jews as well.

Paul is the only major apostle not to have personally known Jesus. He is responsible for many of the New Testament's letters, written to congregations of Jesus followers and embodying teaching and ethical instruction. Paul, who was Jewish himself, focused on bringing the message of Jesus to non-Jews around the Roman empire.

Peter was an apostle whose name attaches to two of the New Testament letters. He focused on bringing the message of Jesus to his fellow Jews.

Pharisees and *Sadducees* were two groups among the variety of first-century Jewish sects. Pharisees were populists and were known for developing a variety of traditions to apply the Torah to daily life. Rabbinic Judaism as we know it today is an outgrowth of the Pharisaic movement. Sadducees were priests (as were some Pharisees), in charge of the Temple, frequently thought to be corrupt and in league with Rome, and unpopular. They also opposed the legal innovations of the Pharisees.

The *Mishnah* is a collection of rabbinic legal discussions along with other material compiled about 200 C.E. The *Talmud* consists of the Mishnah plus the much larger discussion of the Mishnah called the *Gemara*. Sometimes "Talmud" refers to the Gemara alone. There are two Talmuds. The Babylonian Talmud was compiled about 550 C.E.; when people speak of *the* Talmud, this is the one they have in mind. There is also a Jerusalem (or Palestinian, or Yerushalmi) Talmud compiled about 450 C.E. In the footnotes, I sometimes refer to individual parts of the Babylonian Talmud called *tractates*.

References to the Talmud (usually in the footnotes) are written like this: *b. Gittin* 43a. The *b.* means the Babylonian Talmud (*y.* would refer to the Jerusalem Talmud, but I do not cite it). *Gittin* is the name of the particular section or tractate. *43a* is the specific location in the tractate (all locations in the Babylonian Talmud are either *a* or *b*; the numbering system in the Jerusalem Talmud is different).

The *Targum* is a collection of Aramaic translations/paraphrases/explanations of the books of the Hebrew Bible. They were likely originally made to help those who spoke the daily language of Aramaic when Hebrew was no longer the *lingua franca*, the common language. There are various Targums that were compiled over centuries, beginning some time B.C.E. and extending through the first millennium C.E.

The *Zohar* is the "textbook" of Jewish mysticism or *kabbalah.* It was written in the 13th c. C.E. though tradition puts its composition in the 2nd c. C.E.

Yeshua is Jesus' name in Hebrew or Aramaic.

Quotations from the *Tanakh* are taken from the 1985 Jewish Publication Society (JPS) translation in the Accordance electronic edition, version 4.0. Quotations from the New Testament are from the *Complete Jewish Bible* (CJB), as found on biblegateway.com. The CJB is a unique translation by David Stern that often replaces traditional English words and names with Hebrew ones. So for example, the CJB uses *talmidim* instead of *disciples*, or names like *Kefa* instead of *Peter*. When citing the CJB, I have usually put clarifying equivalents in brackets, and most such terms are also included in the glossary at the end. When the CJB cites a passage in the New Testament within which a verse from the Tanakh is quoted, the Tanakh reference is in **boldface**.

Note that the CJB regularly uses *Yeshua* instead of *Jesus*. I have chosen to use *Jesus* in the body of the text, however, for two reasons. One, not everyone is familiar with the name Yeshua, but everyone knows who Jesus is. Two, pairing the name *Jesus* with *tikkun olam* is meant to emphasize that *this Jesus*—the name previous generations of Jews despised, the so-called "god of the Gentiles"—really is part and parcel of Jewish history, ethics, and life.

All URLs mentioned in the book were accessed as of August 1, 2018. There is of course no guarantee that they will continue to be accessible in the future.

INTRODUCTION

Green Onions and Superglue

The Jewish people are a diverse bunch.

A few years ago, I learned that Iranian Jews have a custom of hitting one another with green onions during the Passover seder when singing *Dayenu*, the song that reminds us of God's deliverance from Pharaoh. This is apparently meant to simulate the whips of Pharaoh's taskmasters when they goaded the Israelite slaves into working harder.

In the spirit of celebrating Jewish diversity, I once incorporated this custom into an Ashkenazic seder I led. The participants, unused to this novelty, half-heartedly hit the wrists of the person on their right, unsure if whipping people with scallions was silly, undignified, or just plain weird. Like eating horseradish, bitter herbs reminding us of the bitterness of Egyptian slavery, till you turn red in the face isn't weird, right?

Our diversity is not only based on geography, as is the case with Ashkenazic (Eastern and Northern European) and Sephardic (Mediterranean, Iraqi, Irani) Jews.[1] Religiously we are made up of Orthodox, Conservative, Reform and Reconstructionist Jews. Then there are Conservadox Jews, Modern Orthodox Jews, ultra-Orthodox Jews, Jews of no affiliation, kosher Jews, bacon-loving Jews, Jews who invent their own rituals, Republican Jews,

1. Technically, Iraqi and Irani Jews are *Mizrachi*, or Eastern, but Ashkenazim tend to lump them with the Sephardic Jews. After all, from the viewpoint of European Jews, the Sephardim and the Mizrachim were both "somewhere over there."

Democratic Jews, religious Jews, atheistic Jews, agnostic Jews, Buddhist Jews ("JUBUs"), HinJews—and on it goes.

Amid this diversity (which reflects the increasingly diverse nature of the world at large) there is also an underlying bond that cements us all together. One of those elements in this bond is the set of Jewish values that most of us hold in common.

Whether someone is a radically secular Jew or a traditional, go-to-shul-every-Sabbath Jew, we all tend to agree on certain ethical values, even if we differ on the details. Honor for parents (*kibbud av va'em*) is written into the Jewish DNA, though we express it differently. The value of hospitality (*hakhnasat orchim*) cuts across religious and geographical boundaries, even if some draw the line at letting Aunt Tessie stay over and others actively look to invite strangers into their homes or their *sukkah*. Care for widows and orphans has always ranked high on the Jewish ethical list, as has the tradition of giving to charity (*tzedakah*).

Currently, *tikkun olam* is the Jewish value trending highest. It literally means "repair of the world" but for liberal Jews has come to refer to social action (which betters or "repairs" the world). More traditional Jews may or may not agree that we should be out working for famine relief, but they too agree that the world needs repair, albeit achieved via a different route. The ethical values remain; the details differ.

While Jews may disagree on matters such as the importance of the Talmud, the observance of Jewish holidays, or the existence of God, when push comes to shove we are arguably more bound by our ethics than by anything else. Some may take the view that we are inseparably bound together because God created us as a special people, though atheistic Jews won't accept that premise. Ethics, on the other hand, is something that we could probably get Jews of all stripes to agree is the Jewish Superglue.

Jesus, Jewish Values and Your Mother

The careful reader and probably all other readers too, will notice that the title of this book includes the name of Jesus. Jewish ethics may be the Superglue that binds us together, but Jesus may well bind the Jewish people together for a different reason. When Jews can agree on little else, we generally have agreed that Jesus "is not for us."

Here again we encounter diversity. Jews have voiced the opinions that Jesus was a deceiver, a false prophet, a martyr, the first Reform Jew, a good teacher, a bad teacher, a prophet, a myth, an invention—and regardless of the choice, "not for us." I must add the view of a scholar named John Allegro, though he was not Jewish. Allegro believed that Jesus was a mushroom. What I mean is that his followers were alleged to have smoked something and thereby came up with the whole story. I had to tell you that. I couldn't have made that one up.

In recent years, Jewish scholars, such as Daniel Boyarin, Amy-Jill Levine and others, have explored the idea that even if Jesus is not a fit object of faith for Jews, he is part of the Jewish people. His life and teaching reflect Jewish life of the first-century C.E. They and others would argue that if Jesus is not "for" us, he is definitely "of" us and the sooner we can recover the Jewishness of Jesus, the sooner we can end anti-Semitic stereotypes surrounding Jesus and the New Testament and enhance Jewish-Christian relations.

Hence, this book melds the themes of Jewish values and Jesus. I personally accept that there is a place for Jesus in Jewish life. Many would agree that understanding the Jewishness of Jesus can enhance relations between Christians and Jews. But I think there is more to it than that.

For I am Jewish, and I also believe that Jesus is the Messiah for both Jews and non-Jews. I wrote this book because I am fascinated with how traditional Jewish values show up not only in the Hebrew Bible (where most of them originated), not only in Jewish tradition and modern life, but also in the New Testament.

Part of what it means to say that Jesus and the New Testament are "of us" lies in their reflection of and participation in these universal Jewish values.

The plan of this book is to devote each chapter to a particular value that the Jewish community holds in common. Quite a few other Jewish values could have been added, but I have kept the choice to a workable number.

The New Testament and its central character Jesus exemplify these values. Through an exploration of these values and their place in the New Testament, I hope to add to the conversation in which the New Testament is portrayed as a Jewish book and Jesus as someone that Jews should come to know rather than avoid.

And as for the title of this section—after you finish this book, maybe your mother would enjoy reading it, too!

Which leads us into the first chapter.

CHAPTER 1

THE LIFE AND TIMES OF *Tikkun Olam*

(Repairing the World)

Since this book is called *The Day Jesus Did Tikkun Olam*, which includes a term with which not everyone is familiar, it would be good to know exactly what it was that Jesus did. And for that matter, what the Jewish community does when it "does tikkun olam," which for many, especially for liberal and secular Jews, has become the Jewish value *par excellence*.

So before unpacking what happened when Jesus did tikkun olam, we'll take a journey and explore what it is has meant to others: the life and times of tikkun olam. And a fascinating life it is.

Tikkun olam literally means "repair of the world." In practice it has come to mean working for social justice and betterment. Are you feeding the poor? Then you are doing tikkun olam. Picking up litter along the highway? Tikkun olam. Working to abolish child slavery? Also, tikkun olam. Noted author and rabbi Joseph Telushkin wrote that "Judaism believes that the purpose of Jewish existence is nothing less than 'to perfect the world under the rule of God.'"[1]

Yet doing tikkun olam is not narrowly Jewish nor is it recent. Upton Sinclair's exposé of the meatpacking industry in the 1906 novel *The Jungle* would count as tikkun olam, as would Jacob Riis' 1890 exploration of tenement life, *How the Other Half Lives*.

1. Joseph Telushkin, *Jewish Literacy: The Most Important Things to Know About the Jewish Religion, Its People and Its History* (New York: William Morrow, 1991), p. 549.

Today the term has become entrenched in American discourse, spreading beyond the Jewish community as though the pastrami from the deli overflowed into the Indian buffet next door.

It is the near-ubiquity of the phrase that led Yale University's Jewish president Peter Salovey to tell the graduating class of 2015 a joke about "an American traveling to Israel to work in an orphanage. He is met by his cousin at the airport. After exchanging greetings, the American asks his Israeli cousin, 'How do you say *tikkun olam* in Hebrew?'"[2] Salovey broadened the net beyond the Jewish world in his commencement speech when he told the assembled seniors, "Your purpose in life as a graduate from Yale is simply this: to improve the world. In the Jewish tradition, this is called *tikkun olam*, literally to repair the world."

And so Temple Isaiah of Los Angeles has a web page[3] on tikkun olam, listing the synagogue's programs for fighting human trafficking, helping the homeless, joining the "Green Team," providing groceries, and more.

Going further, the term has also embraced ethical investing. New Yorker Jeremy Balkin, originally from Australia, has been dubbed the "Anti-Wolf of Wall Street," in a nod to the movie starring Leonardo DiCaprio. Balkin is Modern Orthodox and is an investor concerned with the ethics of his profession. "I've been on a journey ever since I gave a TED talk about using financial services and capital to, dare I say, repair the world—tikkun olam," as he is quoted in the *The New York Jewish Week*.[4] (Apparently the world was not the only thing in need of repairing. According to the same article, Balkin "has an 8 inch titanium plate, 14 screws in his left arm and 2 screws in his left leg from sporting injuries in Australia." *Tikkun Balkin*.)

---

2. Yair Rosenberg, "Yale President Calls on Graduates to Commit to Tikkun Olam," www.tabletmag.com/scroll/191120/yale-president-peter-salovey-calls-on-graduates-to-commit-to-tikkun-olam
3. "Tikkun Olam," templeisaiah.com/tikkun-olam.php
4. Jonathan Mark, "Jeremy Balkin, 31," www.thejewishweek.com/special-sections/36-under-36/tikkun-olam-wall-street-jeremy-balkin-31

Whether for Jews or for humanity in general, tikkun olam has become a stand-in for non-negotiable social responsibilities. At least among most American Jews who are Reform, secular and/or left-leaning, it has come to define the Jewish *raison d'être* (though the concept has its detractors, too, especially among some of the more religious). Sylvia Barack Fishman describes it as a "central organizing principle of Jewishness," edging out the place that socialism once occupied for Jews.[5]

The Birth of Tikkun Olam

As with *lashon hara* (chapter 4), the concept of tikkun olam, if not the phrase itself, is found in the Jewish Bible.

"For I have singled him out," says God in reference to Abraham, "that he may instruct his children and his posterity to keep the way of the Lord by doing what is just and right, in order that the Lord may bring about for Abraham what He has promised him."[6]

King David wrote a psalm encouraging us to "shun evil and do good, seek amity and pursue it."[7]

The prophet Isaiah advises, "Thus said the Lord: Observe what is right and do what is just."[8]

The Hebrew Bible did not leave it to the imagination to decide what "doing what is just" meant; the entire Law, embodying the Jewish values we have been looking at throughout this book, spells out what doing the right thing means. From the day Israel received the Torah at Mount Sinai, until now, tikkun olam has been part and parcel of the Jewish DNA.

The Case of the Curious Divorce

The phrase "tikkun olam" itself dates to the early centuries C.E. when the Mishnah—a compendium of Jewish law that forms

5. Sylvia Barack Fishman, *The Way into the Varieties of Jewishness* (Woodstock, VT: Jewish Lights Publishing, 2007), Kindle edition, location 1919.
6. Genesis 18:19.
7. Psalm 34:15. Verse 14 in other English translations.
8. Isaiah 56:1.

the first, and smaller, section of the Talmud—was compiled. Surprisingly, for those who think of tikkun olam in terms of, say, helping end child slavery, the term was originally used in the context of divorce. (And no, the idea was *not* that getting out of a bad marriage would improve the world!) The Mishnah envisioned a quirky scenario, found in *Gittin* 4.

First, though, you need to know that divorce in the days of the Mishnah was accomplished by means of a document of divorce called a *get*, still the case for religious Jewish marriages today. (The plural of *get* is *gittin*). The husband, let's call him Irving Fishman, sends a messenger to deliver the get to his wife. So far, so good. When she receives the get, they will be divorced. But as the agent is en route, Mr. Fishman gets cold feet, changes his mind and sends a second message that he wants to remain married. If the get arrives at Mrs. Fishman's mailbox before the second message does, is she still legally married or not? Since her husband changed his mind, it stands to reason that they are still a married couple. But she doesn't *know* that her husband changed his mind because that message hasn't yet made it through the mails. So, between messages, she might meet Solomon Schneckendorf, remarry and find herself with two husbands at once—and the prospect of having a child by the second man, which carried a multitude of legal and social implications and particularly for the child involved.[9]

Other details crop up and long story short, Rabban Gamaliel rules that if the second message arrived after the get, the divorce was final, plain and simple. The reason for this ruling? "For the sake of tikkun olam," the Mishnah tells us. For the betterment of the world. While this ruling didn't repair the world overall and may seem rather unreasonable to us today, it certainly helped the world of Jewish women at the time. Their marital status would be clear and unambiguous, as would the status of her children. In that culture, in which clearly demarcating such things was of great importance,

9. Of course, this assumes a process slow enough to allow Mrs. Fishman to head to a singles bar, meet a man, and get married between messages. If the Mishnah had been compiled in the days of e-mail, this particular problem would likely not present itself.

this counted for making the world a better place. Furthermore, if a woman could remarry without worrying about whether she was free to do so or not (that is, whether she was still married to someone or not), she would also secure her own livelihood.

Score one for tikkun olam.

Another early example of tikkun olam is related to the first. What if the husband used the name Irving Fishman when in Israel, but when traveling on business to Turkey, he went by Slapsie Maxie Hungerman? (Changing names is not uncommon. In modern times, David Ben-Gurion was born David Grün and many Jews who made *aliyah* have altered their names from the originals.[10]) Rabban Gamaliel once again stepped into the fray, ruling that a get had to include—for both husband and wife—all alternative names they used. This again bettered the world of women, because if Irving divorced Mrs. Fishman (his first wife) and Slapsie divorced Mrs. Hungerman (the same person's second wife), nothing would be hidden from the wives—they could both be sure that the same husband was involved and again, their marital status would become clear.

Score two for tikkun olam.

From Women to Wall Street

We encounter the idea of tikkun olam in connection with yet another Jewish legal ruling, this time enacted by the famous Rabbi Hillel, who lived in the first century B.C.E. and is also known as Hillel the Great or Hillel the Elder, to distinguish him from various other Hillels.

This Hillel, it turns out, indelibly stamped Jewish life. The Jewish college organization is named after him and he also penned the well-known saying, "If I am not for myself, who is for me? And when I am for myself, what am I? And if not now, when?" The combination sandwich we eat at the seder with both *charoset* and *maror*? Hillel invented it (though he seems to have used only

10. For examples, see en.wikipedia.org/wiki/Hebraization of surnames

maror; what we eat today is a later adaptation, probably from someone who had had enough horseradish and Hillel or no Hillel, was going to sweeten it up some).

Here's what Hillel did for the sake of tikkun olam. This time it involved finances rather than divorce arrangements. In the Bible, every seventh year for the Jewish people in Israel was supposed to be a time for cancelling all monetary debts. This would not begin to fly today, but the Torah was a highly humanitarian document, coupled with the belief that the God who could bring slaves out of Egypt and demolish the Egyptian army could see to it that absolving debts would not ruin a lender's financial situation.

Be that as it may, human nature is what it is. That's why in the Book of Deuteronomy, the last of the Five Books of Moses, we read:

> Beware lest you harbor the base thought, "The seventh year, the year of remission, is approaching," so that you are mean to your needy kinsman and give him nothing. He will cry out to the LORD against you, and you will incur guilt.[11]

For the lender, there was always the prospect of having to loan money knowing in advance that the debt would be forgiven in the sabbatical year. In effect, the loan would be turned into a gift. The lender, then, was meant to trust that God would continue to meet his own needs despite the prospect of no repayment. But there were always some who would refuse to extend a loan as the sabbatical year approached, knowing that, as far as they were concerned, they would be stiffed.

Enter Rabbi Hillel. For the sake of tikkun olam, we read, he enacted a piece of legislation known as *prosbul*.[12] Hillel noticed that in fact, people *were* refusing to loan money as the seventh year

11. Deuteronomy 15:9.

12. *Prosbul* is a Hebrew word that comes via Greek, and to this day there are theories about what it means but no definitive answer. See www.balashon.com/2007/10/prosbul.html

approached. In order to encourage continued lending, which was necessary for the smooth functioning of society, he decreed that loans could be collected even in the seventh year as long as it was done by a court rather than by an individual. Why by a court? In the common understanding of that time, the loans in Deuteronomy 15 only applied to those made and collected by individuals; they did not apply to a group like a court. So, the loan could still be collected by a court and the individual then reimbursed.

Among Jewish commentators, there has been debate as to whether prosbul violated the spirit as well as the letter of the commandment that loans should not be collected during the seventh year. Undoubtedly, Hillel's motives were noble: he wanted to mitigate the sin of not extending loans by choosing something that seemed to be the lesser of two evils. His decree left some uneasy; some later rabbis practically *plotzed* and "expressed their astonishment at the fact that Hillel dared to abrogate the Mosaic institution of the release of all debts every seventh year."[13] Nevertheless, Hillel made his stunning ruling "for the sake of tikkun olam." In this case, it was the world of poor people that was "repaired," for the decree ensured that those who needed loans just to get by would not be overlooked as the seventh year approached.

Score three for tikkun olam.

Tikkun Olam Meets *The Electric Kool-Aid Acid Test*[14]

It should be a straight line from the idea of bettering the lot of women and poor people to the modern idea of social action. The exact shape would look different today, but if you can better the "world" of women and the poor, it's a short step to bettering the world in general.

---

13. *Jewish Encyclopedia* (1906), www.jewishencyclopedia.com, under "Prosbul."

14. This refers to a 1968 book of the same name by Tom Wolfe, describing the real-life adventures of a group of travelers who used psychedelic drugs.

Unfortunately, life is rarely a straight line and the idea of tikkun olam took a detour before arriving at the modern conception. As it turns out, it's a detour that has ended up resonating with many people.

The detour occurred in the Middle Ages, specifically in the 16th century in the town of Safed, located in the Galilee area of Israel. The key player here is Jerusalem-born Rabbi Isaac Luria, who is known for developing a certain kind of *kabbalah*. And what exactly is kabbalah? It is usually described as Jewish mysticism and it was in full bloom in the Middle Ages, having existed in one form or another even earlier. Traditionally study of the kabbalah and its main textbook, the *Zohar*, was reserved for those over forty years of age.

No longer. As with cottage cheese and yogurt, we now have both the traditional full-fat and lo-cal versions of kabbalah, old school and new school. "Kabbalah-lite" has entered mainstream culture through pop followers like Madonna and through the Kabbalah Centre, a Los Angeles-based organization that attempts to disseminate the teachings of kabbalah worldwide at a popular level. "Australian supermodel Miranda Kerr revealed during a recent interview that she keeps in her purse a copy of The Zohar," reports *The Algemeiner*.

> The former Victoria's Secret model told Beauticate.com that the book of "healing and protection" is one of the essential items she always keeps in her handbag, along with a hairbrush, sunglasses, headphones and a bracelet made by her son, Flynn. During the interview, she read out loud an excerpt from the book that explains its ability to "keep darkness from coming near you."[15]

If you've read about people who wear a red string, that's kabbalah. If you've heard stories about the Frankenstein-like

15. Shiryn Solny, "Christian Supermodel Miranda Kerr Says She Keeps Mystical Jewish Text in Her Handbag for a 'Little Protection'," www.algemeiner.com/2016/08/04/christian-supermodel-miranda-kerr-keeps-mystical-jewish-text-in-her-handbag-for-a-little-protection-video/

creature called the *golem*, whose clay form came to life when the Hebrew word *emet* (truth) was written on its forehead and who existed to protect Jews, that too is kabbalah (though more of the old school variety).

Isaac Luria's kabbalah is known as—no surprise—"Lurianic Kabbalah." What Luria did was to reboot the kabbalah by developing his own version, which is the one that has captured the popular imagination. For many, even if they have no idea who Luria is, kabbalah means his version and no other. I am guessing that this is because it brings a kind of "mythological" as well as mystical approach to reality. For if the *Zohar* is the basic book of kabbalah, Luria created the big-screen adaptation. Lurianic Kabbalah offers an explanation for how the universe came to be, why there is evil in the world and how the world, crippled as it is with sin and evil, can be repaired. Or in other words, how we can do tikkun olam.

Here is Lurianic Kabbalah in sixty seconds:

- God-in-Himself is known as the *Ein Sof*, meaning "Without End."
- By means of *tzimtum*, or "contraction" into Himself, God enabled the creation of the universe.
- Furthermore, via ten emanations or *sefirot*, God interacts with his creation; the sefirot have a complex relationship to one another and to the world. You may have seen kabbalistic diagrams depicting the "Ten Sefirot").
- When God created the universe, divine sparks were encased in shells or vessels which somehow broke open, causing the sparks to fall to earth.
- From that moment (known as the *shevirat kelim* or "breaking of the vessels"), evil has entered the world.
- It is now incumbent on all Jews to perform the mitzvot, or commandments, in order to raise the sparks and bring about—you guessed it—tikkun olam, the restoration of the universe.

To simplify all this: there is first of all the creation of the universe, which was originally a good place; then came the fall of "divine sparks" to earth which introduced evil into the world (sort of a Jewish Pandora's Box); and finally there is the mandate that through observing the mitzvot, the commandments of Judaism, we can raise the sparks back to God and repair the world.

Nowhere in the Bible is the world described in such strange, almost psychedelic, terms. Nowhere do the Scriptures speak of divine sparks falling to earth, cosmic vessels breaking open, or raising sparks back to God. Kabbalah, as far as we can tell, came from other sources than Scripture.

To those unfamiliar with Luria's unlikely vision of the universe, the whole thing sounds like someone has been smoking something, perhaps something like a *Dr. Strange* movie and suspiciously un-Jewish. Yet to others, this is Jewish mythology that captures the imagination with a lot of explanatory power. In an age of *Star Wars* and *Lord of the Rings*, for many people, mythology seems to be just what the Jewish doctor ordered: "For relief of confusion about life, take Lurianic Kabbalah!" More simply, it resonates with the impulse that many have to be "spiritual."

The continuity with the earlier idea of tikkun olam is clear: to repair this broken world, we need to do the commandments, the mitzvot, many of which have to do with social improvement. But in Lurianic Kabbalah, the canvas on which tikkun olam is painted has morphed from the everyday world of home and work to a strange, cosmic scenario.

Most Jews today are probably of a less mystical bent and when they speak of tikkun olam, they have in mind the sorts of things we saw at the beginning of this chapter: social projects, ending exploitation, working for economic equality. And so we have come full circle in exploring the life and times of tikkun olam. Or almost. Because we now need to have a look at how this value of "repairing the world" shows up in the New Testament and the life of Jesus.

CHAPTER 2

HONOR OF FATHER AND MOTHER

(Kibbud Av va'Em)

In the 1989 film *New York Stories*, Woody Allen managed to take the stereotype of the overbearing Jewish mother to a new level. In a rather unsettling visual, his character's mother suddenly appears in the sky, to be forevermore a presence in his life, a continual offeror of advice and a nag—in full view of the entire city, no less.

As if to atone for the unflattering image of the domineering mother, Jewish culture has also preserved another attitude in which Jews profess undying love and closeness to our mothers: think of the numerous renditions of the song "My Yiddishe Momma" or Al Jolson's performance of "My Mammy" in the film *The Jazz Singer*, in which he portrayed fictional Jewish singer Jakie Rabinowitz.[1]

Despite our conflicted responses to our mothers (and fathers), many of us end up helping our parents through their advancing years, aiding them in settling into independent or assisted living communities, clearing the path through the maze of finances, medical needs and government regulations. What we don't do is abandon them, whether they are nagging us from the sky or not.

The responsibility Jews feel towards their parents can be traced back to the Bible. "Honor your father and your mother"

1. For some reason, fathers have not figured as prominently in the popular Jewish imagination.

is one of the Ten Commandments. The book of Proverbs waxes more poetic:

> My son, heed the discipline of your father,
> And do not forsake the instruction of your mother;
> For they are a graceful wreath upon your head,
> A necklace about your throat. [2]

Despite the Allen-esque relationships some of us sustain with our mothers—on Jweekly.com, Jonathan Rubin advises the liberal, largely secular Jewish community of the San Francisco area to "Honor thy mother, even if she's a meddler"[3]—the imperative to show honor to our parents is still alive and well among Jews.

The most visible example of the importance of this value is the widespread network of Jewish retirement communities. According to the Association of Jewish Aging Services, as of 2012 there were some 100 non-profit Jewish senior organizations and 130 senior communities in the United States[4] (most of which generally welcome non-Jews as well).

Amy Hershberg Lederman, writing in the *Arizona Jewish Post*, tells her readers that "The positive commandment to honor requires us to provide food, shelter, clothing and the type of support and care that our parents gave us when we were young, especially as they age."[5] This is not always easy.

I recently read *A Bittersweet Season: Caring for Our Aging Parents—and Ourselves* by Jewish *New York Times* writer Jane Gross. She chronicles her and her brother's part in managing the caregiving of their mother through transitions, medical issues and

---

2. Proverbs 1:8–9.
3. J. Correspondent [Jonathan Rubin], "Honor Thy Mother, Even If Shes [*sic*] a Meddler," www.jweekly.com/article/full/29210/honor-thy-mother-even-if-she-s-a-meddler
4. Alyssa Gerace, "Exploring Senior Living Niches: Jewish Retirement Communities," bitly.com/retirecom
5. Amy Hirshberg Lederman, "Honor Your Parents—And Believe in Them," www.azjewishpost.com/2010/honor-your-parents----and-believe-in-them/

their own stressed-out lives.[6] Difficult or not, many would not think of abandoning their parents in their time of need.

Like the other core values in this book, this one—known in Hebrew as *kibbud av va'em*—is ingrained in the Jewish way of life. The Talmud, obscure for many Jews but full of ethical insights, tells us that we should honor our parents just as we honor God. Why? Because all three were partners together in creating our lives.[7] Even an atheist gets the idea: we owe our lives to our parents.

Your Mother, Your Father and Alfred Hitchcock

The insistence on honoring parents is seen especially in two books of the Bible. The first is Deuteronomy, which encapsulates the law God is giving to the nation of Israel when they are on the verge of entering the Promised Land. It is a book rich in ethical insights in which, like bookends, the command to honor father and mother appears near the beginning as well as near the end:

> "Honor your father and your mother, as the Lord your God has commanded you, that you may long endure, and that you may fare well, in the land that the Lord your God is assigning to you." (Deuteronomy 5:16)

That passage combines the command to show honor to parents with a promise of well-being. For many of us today, the well-being may be more internal than anything else. Despite the hardships, we feel good when we can care for our parents. But for the Jewish people of Moses' time, the well-being extended to the externals of a contented life in the land of Israel.

---

6. Jane Gross, *A Bittersweet Season: Caring for Our Aging Parents—and Ourselves* (New York: Alfred A. Knopf, 2011).

7. *b. Kiddushin* 30b: "Our Rabbis taught: There are three partners in man, the Holy One, blessed be He, the father, and the mother. When a man honours his father and his mother, the Holy One, blessed be He, says: 'I ascribe [merit] to them as though I had dwelt among them and they had honoured Me'." (Soncino edition)

The counterpart is found towards the end of the book:

> "Cursed be he who insults his father or mother.—And all the people shall say, Amen."[8]

Here, the opposite of honor is in view, and the people of Israel cite their approval with a word found throughout the Jewish liturgy: "Amen!" meaning roughly, "I agree."

The other book of the Bible that emphasizes honor to one's parents is the book of Proverbs, a collection of pithy sayings, written in poetic form, on a staggeringly diverse number of subjects. This particular topic is found in such proverbs as the following, which I've taken from a larger number on the subject:

> A son who causes shame and disgrace
> Plunders his father, puts his mother to flight.[9]
> One who reviles his father or mother,
> Light will fail him when darkness comes.[10]
> Listen to your father who begot you;
> Do not disdain your mother when she is old.[11]
> He who robs his father and mother and says, "It is no offense,"
> Is a companion to vandals.[12]
> The eye that mocks a father
> And disdains the homage due a mother—
> The ravens of the brook will gouge it out,
> Young eagles will devour it.[13]

---

8. Deuteronomy 27:16.
9. Proverbs 19:26.
10. Proverbs 20:20.
11. Proverbs 23:22.
12. Proverbs 28:24.
13. Proverbs 30:17.

For the most part, with the exception of the third proverb, I seem to have picked proverbs that escalate in intensity as we go along. We move from shame and disgrace to one's light failing, then to being the abettor in crime and finally to the most colorful one of all that brings to mind Alfred Hitchcock's movie *The Birds*.

The star of that film, Tippi Hedren, did not have her eyes pecked out, but another unfortunate person did succumb to the frenzied attacks of the manic birds. I don't know if that person mocked his father or not, but it's an image calculated to keep someone awake at night wondering if they really should have called their father that terrible name.

Being a proverb, the intention is to be a memorable way of saying that what you dish out, you'll get in return. And having read it, you're certain never to look at a pigeon in quite the same way again.

The Day Uncle Murray Visited

"According to the rabbis," writes Rabbi Joseph Telushkin, quoting from Leviticus 19:3, in the third book of the Torah, 'awe' means deep, abiding respect, for example, as in not sitting in one's father's place at the table."[14] That's not quite on the same level as getting Mom and Dad into Mount Sinai Retirement Community. But the rabbis had a point: honor works in small things as well as in larger ones.

In families that still manage to have meals together, people often have their usual places at the dinner table, out of habit if nothing else. That was how I grew up.

In our home, my father sat against the wall with the mural of Venice, my mother was seated with her back to the kitchen for easy access, while the wall behind my seat featured three plastic fish that passed as decorations in the 1960s. And when my grandfather came every Friday evening, he took the otherwise-empty seat nearest the window. (I had no siblings, so our round table worked

14. Telushkin, *Jewish Literacy*, p. 527.

perfectly.) I'm sure had I tried to take my father's seat, I would have been informed that "that's where your father sits." A minor point of honor, perhaps, but honor nonetheless.

Rabbi Telushkin continues with another example of honor: "not siding with a parent's adversary during a dispute."[15] Now that's an interesting one, falling somewhere between seating arrangements and caregiving tasks in the honor-giving hierarchy.

In practical terms, this would mean that if Uncle Murray, or the president of the synagogue, or the *yenta* down the street, has a beef with Dad or Mom, honor means not joining in as prosecuting attorney against our parents—even if they are in the wrong. Of course, this doesn't preclude speaking privately to or about them afterward or doing what we think is right in a less "public" forum. The point is to not shame our parents.

Just when we think Jewish tradition is really making us toe the line, it throws us a curve ball. What honor does *not* include is listening to one's parents in the matter of choosing a marriage partner. This modern-sounding exception, surprisingly enough, actually goes back to the Middle Ages.

With exquisite reason, some rabbis pointed out that if someone marries a person they don't love, they will end up hating that person. That, in turn, would violate the commandment to love one's neighbor as oneself![16] (I suspect, though, that intermarriage, even for love, was not something that the medieval rabbis had in mind. They would surely be aghast at the suggestion that their conclusions should be used in the service of marrying "outside the tribe," love or no love.)

In today's fast-paced lives, when family members often do not even live in proximity, it's not always easy to figure out what honoring parents looks like in practice. It is sometimes easier to see when honor is lacking. One rabbi relates this story:

---

15. Ibid.
16. Ibid., pp. 527–28.

> A man approached Rav Chaim Soloveitchik of Brisk with a question. His father was ill in another city far away. Since there is a machlokes (difference of opinion regarding Jewish law) as to whether one must spend money in order to fulfill the mitzvah of honoring one's parents, he wanted to know whether he was obligated to spend the large sum necessary to take the train to visit his father.
>
> "You are not obligated to spend the money to visit your father," the Rav answered him. "You can walk!"[17]

Commandments and Pickles

Honor for parents may be on the Jewish radar, but not everyone knows that its origin lies in the Ten Commandments. It was different in the first century, when people were well acquainted with the Bible. Jesus could readily assume that knowledge on the part of his hearers, as shown in the following story from the Gospel of Mark. The story begins:

> As he [Jesus] was starting on his way, a man ran up, kneeled down in front of him and asked, "Good rabbi, what should I do to obtain eternal life?"[18]

Mark's writing style tends to be as breathless as a sportscaster. Things always happen "immediately, "straightaway," or "directly," depending on which translation you are reading. In Mark's telling, the man "runs up" to Jesus, intent on getting hold of him just as he takes his first steps out of town. Most of us would be annoyed to be waylaid just as we are about to start something—why did he have to wait till the last minute? Perhaps we should understand that this question had been pressing on the man for some time and as Jesus was about to depart, he realized that getting an answer was either now or never.

---

17. As told in a brochure by Rabbi Jack Abramowitz, *Kibud Av'V'eim* (NCSY Torah on One Foot Series; New York: National Conference of Synagogue Youth, n.d.). Available as a PDF at www.ou.org/torah/attachment/33983

18. Mark 10:17.

The man's question does not always resonate with modern readers, as he asks about "eternal life." I have a file of demographic surveys of the Jewish community and in none of them can I find the word "afterlife." "Heaven" does crop up, but only metaphorically or citing a Bible verse. In one case, Berkeley, California is described as "foodie heaven."[19] But this story takes place in the first century, when ideas of the afterlife were widely accepted. (Orthodox Jews today still believe in an afterlife, but it gets little attention in comparison with the emphasis on living according to Torah in this life.)

Jesus' reply may strike us as a bit strange:

> Yeshua said to him, "Why are you calling me good? No one is good except God! You know the *mitzvot*—'**Don't murder, don't commit adultery, don't steal, don't give false testimony**, don't defraud, **honor your father and mother**...'"[20]

Jesus begins by pointing to the fact that only God is "good" in any ultimate sense. But why would he preface talking about the commandments by saying this? In the culture of the time, the man may have been trying to flatter Jesus, expecting flattery in return.[21] Or the implication may be that since only God is good, people cannot "obtain eternal life" simply by their good deeds, as important as our actions are.[22] That is, it may be an attempt by Jesus to get the man to think more deeply about the relationship between eternal life, human deeds and the commandments. After all, the man admits a little further on that he *has* kept all these commandments, yet he can say, "Where do I still fall short?"[23] In

---

19. Lisa Alcalay Klug, "Top Ten Jewish Neighborhoods," lisaklug.com/articles-2/arts-culture/jewish-living-magazine-cover-story/

20. Mark 10:18-19. Boldface original. Boldface in the CJB translation is meant to indicate that the bolded portion is a quotation from the Hebrew Bible.

21. Ben Witherington III, *The Gospel of Mark: A Socio-rhetorical Commentary* (Grand Rapids, MI: Eerdmans, 2001), p. 282.

22. Ibid., citing Larry Hurtado, *Mark* (New York: Harper & Row, 1983), p. 151.

23. Matthew 19:20, in a slightly different telling of the same story.

other words, he had a felt need. In any event, he quotes five of the ten commandments—the ones that have to do with how we treat others. (The first five concern how we relate to God.)

Notice how Jesus continues: "You know the mitzvot," the commandments. First-century Jews had the Ten Commandments at their first-century fingertips. On the other hand, if Jesus were speaking today, he might well need to ask, "*Do* you know the commandments?" In 2007, Reuters reported a survey conducted by the firm of Kelton Research.[24] The fascinating if somewhat disturbing results of the survey showed that 80% of respondents knew that a Big Mac contains "two all-beef patties," but less than 60% knew the commandment, "Do not murder." Sixty-two percent remembered that a Big Mac comes with a pickle, while only 45% knew "Honor your father and mother." And 25% of Americans knew *all* the Big Mac ingredients (which for the record are "two all-beef patties, special sauce, lettuce, cheese, pickles, onions on a sesame seed bun") compared with 14% who could name all the Ten Commandments.[25]

While the survey's line of questioning might have been a bit of a set-up (like comparing apples and oranges, or commandments and pickles), it does show that what Jesus assumed his hearers knew back then is not necessarily what they would know today.

But now, having read this far, like first-century Jews you also know about the commandment to honor your parents.

Parents, Children and Aretha Franklin

Jesus is not the only one in the New Testament to quote the commandment about honoring parents. Paul was one of Jesus' early followers who brought his Jewish upbringing to the task of engaging non-Jews over the question of whether Jesus was the Messiah.

---

24. "Americans Know Big Macs Better than Ten Commandments," www.reuters.com/article/2007/10/12/us-bible-commandments-idUSN1223894020071012

25. Melanie B. Smith, "Can You Name All 10?" legacy.decaturdaily.com/decaturdaily/religion/071027/ten.shtml

Writing to a group of Jesus' followers in the city of Ephesus, located in what today is western Turkey, he quotes the same commandment. Most believers in Jesus in this city were non-Jews. Many, though, would have been familiar with the synagogue and the Hebrew Bible because throughout the Diaspora there was a substantial presence of gentiles in the synagogue who worshiped alongside Jews without taking the full step of converting to Judaism. (These synagogue-friendly Gentiles were known as "God-fearers.") And so, Paul restates the commandment to honor one's parents:

> Children, what you should do in union with the Lord is obey your parents, for this is right. **"Honor your father and mother"**—this is the first commandment that embodies a promise—**"so that it may go well with you, and you may live long in the Land."**[26]

In Aretha Franklin's song, she belted out "R-E-S-P-E-C-T, find out what it means to me," for good measure adding, "Sock it to me, sock it to me." As we saw in Deuteronomy, the Bible's command for parental honor and respect comes with its own sock-it-to-me in the form of a promise from God, as Paul points out. Moses was referring to having a long life in the land of Israel. Paul, writing to those far from Israel, paraphrases "in the land" as "on earth." And the fact is, that whether one is in Israel, New York, or Duluth those blessed with good family relationships instead of parental or spousal abuse, extreme sibling rivalry, or poisoned communications do in fact enjoy better long-term emotional and mental health, which affects physical well-being—to put a modern spin on it.

For good measure, Paul also advises parents to treat their children well.

> Fathers, don't irritate your children and make them resentful; instead, raise them with the Lord's kind of discipline and guidance.[27]

Honor and respect are indeed two-way streets.

---

26. Ephesians 6:1-3. Boldface original.
27. Ephesians 6:4.

Putting it Into Practice

Jesus' affirmation of the commandment to honor one's parents can be seen in the provision he made for his own mother prior to his death:

> When Yeshua saw his mother and the *talmid* [disciple] whom he loved standing there, he said to his mother, "Mother, this is your son." Then he said to the *talmid*, "This is your mother." And from that time on, the *talmid* took her into his own home.[28]

With no Hebrew Homes for the Aged, it fell to family members to directly care for their aging parents. So Jesus—who died in his early thirties far in advance of the usual life expectancy—provides for "continuing care" for his mother by assigning her to one of his followers. We can assume that she was not yet in advanced age; but nevertheless, she had need of a home and a surrogate "son" to help her through the rest of her life.

Avoiding the Task

Nevertheless, then as now, not everyone upheld the spirit of honoring parents: remember the story recounted earlier about the man who didn't want to spend train fare to visit his ill father. Caring for one's aging father or mother is no easy job—and perhaps even harder today, when institutions have replaced families as the leading provider of such care, which means vetting nursing homes or assisted living communities, monitoring the care given, travelling distances and much more.

And so, at one point, Jesus confronted those whom he felt were neglecting the basic duty of honoring their parents.

> Indeed," he said to them, "you have made a fine art of departing from God's command in order to keep your tradition!"[29]

Jesus, it must be said, was not opposed to Jewish tradition or to any and all traditions. In the New Testament we see him as a

---

28. John 19:26-27.
29. Mark 7:9.

regular participant in Jewish life: attending the synagogue, reading and speaking on the *haftarah* (or its first-century equivalent), observing Passover and Sukkot, visiting the Temple in Jerusalem. (As they say, it's all about upbringing: his parents, religious Jews both, gave him a *bris*—circumcision—at eight days and a few weeks later, the ancient version of a *pidyon ha-ben*—the ceremony of redeeming the first-born[30]). Jesus was not exercised over tradition, but over particular traditions that he believed were "setting aside the commands of God."

> For Moshe [Moses] said, '**Honor your father and your mother,**' and '**Anyone who curses his father or mother must be put to death.**' But you say, 'If someone says to his father or mother, "I have promised as a *korban*"' (that is, as a gift to God) '"what I might have used to help you,"' then you no longer let him do anything for his father or mother.[31]

Let's unpack this. Besides the commandment to "honor your father and your mother," there were also commandments that I have not mentioned until now, which concern putting to death those who curse father and mother. This comes across as unbearably harsh to modern readers.

The Hebrew Bible's legal code, though, was on a par with other legal codes of the time and often an improvement. And in fact, in many cases monetary payment was made in lieu of the death penalty. So, the "death-penalty" commandments are really meant to underscore the seriousness of the violation.

For all but the most egregious violations of humanity, we are to imagine a large yellow warning sign rather than *Alice in Wonderland*'s Red Queen shouting, "Off with their heads!" In any event, Bible scholars agree that something much more serious than a teenager's "the heck with you" is in mind by "cursing" one's parents.

Back to the story.

---

30. This ceremony is observed today only by the religious. It involves giving a number of silver coins to a *kohen*, or someone descended from priests, in order to "redeem" a firstborn son.
31. Mark 7:10-12.

Everyone Jesus spoke too agreed that the Bible taught honor to parents. Then as now, however, there were some legal loopholes that allowed unscrupulous (or lazy) people a way out.

Let's imagine someone that we'll call Manny. Manny decides to donate his old bedroom dresser, which otherwise could have been sold or used, to the Temple in Jerusalem. The dresser would be physically labeled with the Hebrew word "Korban," in this context meaning "given to God." (Think of labeling your boxes on moving day "for the kitchen," "for the den." These items were "for the Temple.")

According to one school of thought, now that the dresser was "for the Temple," no one else could use it, including family members. Maybe Manny just didn't want his dresser to go his parents. Maybe it was less work to just give it to the Temple. Maybe he wanted to appear "religious" or wanted to be well thought of. Or conversely, maybe he made the gift to the Temple, then wanted to reclaim it for his parents' needs—and was told, sorry, donations aren't returned.

Either way, Jesus calls out such people, whether the donor or the Temple bureaucracy, for neglecting to ensure that parents would be honored.[32]

> "Thus, with your tradition which you had handed down to you, you nullify the Word of God! And you do other things like this."[33]

Jesus concludes, without going into detail, that his listeners have other traditions with equal effect. We should be clear: honor of parents was ingrained in Jewish life and most people did the right thing in this regard. But there were some who didn't, or who tried and were stymied by the system.

I'm sure Jesus would have been glad to meet your mother and mine and a good conversation would ensue over hummus, chicken

32. For more details about *korban*, see John R. Donahue and Daniel J. Harrington, *The Gospel of Mark* (Collegeville, MN: The Liturgical Press, 2005), p. 223, nn. 11, 12. They suggest that a vow was made upon donating the korban gift, creating a conflict between honoring one's vow and honoring one's parents.

33. Mark 7:13; see also Matthew 15:3-6

necks, or Chinese food—depending on what your own mother's favorite food is. He would have wanted to be sure, though, that you showed her the honor due her!

A Final Word

Some have pointed out that there are times when Jesus' teaching seems at variance with his advocacy of Jewish values, such as honor for parents. What are we to make of something like the following?

> Do you think that I [Jesus] have come to bring peace in the Land? Not peace, I tell you, but division! For from now on, a household of five will be divided, three against two, two against three.
> Father will be divided against son
> and **son against father**,
> mother against daughter
> and **daughter against mother**,
> mother-in-law against her daughter-in-law
> and **daughter-in-law against mother-in-law**."[34]

Jesus and the Royal Tenenbaums

In the above passage, Jesus seems to violate the value of honor of father and mother. He makes the rather disturbing statement that he will be the cause of massive family dysfunction, something on the order of *The Royal Tenenbaums* on steroids. This is one seriously messed up family: sons are against fathers and daughters are antagonistic to mothers (so much for honoring parents), the in-laws are yelling at each other and it's doubtful that the five people in this family will be sitting down to dinner together anytime soon. In fact, why would the gospel writers even include such a passage in a book about someone whom Christians call the "Prince of Peace"?

Jesus' listeners, attuned as they were in those days to the Bible, would have recognized that Jesus was quoting from the prophet

34. Luke 12:51-53. Boldface original. See also Matthew 10:34-36.

Micah. Micah wrote some 600 years before Jesus and he spoke of his own day and age in similar terms:

> Trust no friend,
> Rely on no intimate;
> Be guarded in speech
> With her who lies in your bosom.
> For son spurns father,
> Daughter rises up against mother,
> Daughter-in-law against mother-in-law—
> A man's own household
> Are his enemies.[35]

Micah was describing the disintegration of society at a time when the Jewish people were about to be besieged by a foreign nation and exiled into Babylon for seventy years. Society was a moral mess; in fact the prophets attributed the exile to Babylon to the sins of both Israel's leaders and the people they led.

Jewish tradition applied this same picture of societal meltdown to the period of the Messiah's arrival. Jesus was not telling his listeners that family dysfunction was desirable. But what would happen was that some in a given family would choose to follow Jesus as the Messiah and others would not. Unlike, say, the decision to order pastrami over corned beef, that choice would often strain family relationships.

Given that there were serious disputes in the first century Jewish community over Jesus, not to mention the fact that the Roman authorities did not look fondly on any messianic movement, loyalties could easily be divided between Jesus, synagogue, family, Rome and others. Kibbud av va'em could easily end up taking a back seat to other options.

To seemingly make matters worse, we also have these passages:

> To another he [Jesus] said, "Follow me!" but the man replied, "Sir, first let me go away and bury my father." Yeshua said, "Let the dead bury their own dead; you, go and proclaim the Kingdom of God!" Yet another said, "I

35. Micah 7:5-6.

> will follow you, sir, but first let me say good-by to the people at home." To him Yeshua said, "No one who puts his hand to the plow and keeps looking back is fit to serve in the Kingdom of God."[36]
>
> "Whoever loves his father or mother more than he loves me is not worthy of me; anyone who loves his son or daughter more than he loves me is not worthy of me."[37]

Again, all is not quite what it seems at first glance. Once more we find help from the Hebrew Bible:

> [Each member of the tribe of Levi] … said of his father and mother,
> "I consider them not."
> His brothers he disregarded,
> Ignored his own children.
> Your precepts alone they observed,
> And kept Your covenant.[38]

This refers to an incident in Exodus 32:25-29, when following the idolatrous disaster of making the Golden Calf, the Levites obeyed God by killing 3,000 of their fellow Israelites (we'll leave the rather large ethical problem to the side for now). Moses is not saying that the Levites had no concern for their own parents, nor that they literally failed to recognize their children. Moses is praising the tribe in hyperbolic terms to underscore that family bonds did not take precedence over God's requirements. In less dramatic circumstances than the story from Exodus, it still takes mature love rather than hatred to show honor to one's mother and father yet to give precedence to God's requirements.

In other words, Jewish values were not and are not now, absolute. For people of faith, how to live out those values requires making ethical decisions in a variety of situations. Jesus' apparent exceptions, then, were born of just such decision-making as we find in the Hebrew Bible as well.

---

36. Luke 9:59-62; see also Matthew 8:21-22.
37. Matthew 10:37.
38. Deuteronomy 33:9.

CHAPTER 3

IS IT GOOD FOR THE JEWS?

(*Kiddush Hashem* and *Chillul Hashem*)

In 2009, an online article appeared entitled "The Chillul Hashem of A-Rod."[1] If you don't know what a "chillul Hashem" is, you're not alone and you'll find out in a moment.

Alexander Rodriguez, formerly of the New York Yankees and aka A-Rod, is not Jewish himself but has been involved with the famous Kabbalah Center, whose kabbalah-lite teaching has attracted the interest of other celebrities, including Madonna. When his steroid usage from 2001 to 2003 came to light, A-Rod admitted to using the drugs—the admission allegedly coming forth while he wore the Kabbalah Centre's red string around his wrist. Despite this admission of guilt, Rabbi Michael Green, author of the above-mentioned article, opined that his actions "will be viewed by many as another 'strike' against the Jews. At the end of the day, I wish that Alex would end his infatuation with this 'religion' and do his part to keep anything that might appear even remotely Jewish out of his spotlight."

Considering this story, one might think that *chillul Hashem* means something like, "it's bad for the Jews." That's not a bad guess, though the phrase actually means "the desecration of God" (*HaShem*, "the Name," being a traditional way of referring to

1. rabbimichaelgreen.com/blog/2009/02/26/a-rods-chillul-hashem/?nl201310, no longer online.

God). The idea is that when we act wrongly, we dishonor God who would want us to act otherwise. In practice, it has come to also mean an action that reflects poorly on the Jewish people and by extension, on the God of the Jews.

Its opposite is *kiddush Hashem*, the sanctification or honoring of God's name, which has similarly come to mean something that reflects well on Jewish people (though such acts hardly get commented on as much as acts that *don't* reflect well on us). Kiddush Hashem has also come to mean martyrdom; but more on that later.

Let's see what else might be good or bad for the Jews, besides A-Rod. Can driving your car be good for the Jews? Or conversely, bad? According to one writer, the answer is that it could be both:

> On many occasions, I've had the good fortune of driving through Westchester County with my rabbi, and have noticed that he is a fairly cautious and courteous driver. Being from New York City, I found this somewhat unusual, and once asked him why he drives so cautiously. He replied that should he race a yellow light while wearing a *kippah* (skullcap), or forget to signal a lane change, he wouldn't be making a statement about himself only as a driver, but also as a Jew and, for some, about all Jews. In this way, he would bring dishonor to God and to the Jewish people, thereby committing an act of Hillul HaShem.[2] That's why he always tries to drive cautiously and courteously.[3]

Being also from New York City—and having taken my driving lessons at Columbus Circle—I've thought that driving like a mad cabbie could actually be a mark of honor, which in some circles might actually *enhance* the image of Jews. But point taken, though

---

2. Hebrew and Yiddish terms are variously spelled in English. Chillul ha-Shem, chillul haShem, Hillul HaShem or hillul ha-Shem, etc. etc.

3. Elliot Forchheimer, "Does It Really Matter How I Drive?," www.myjewishlearning.com/texts/Bible/Weekly_Torah_Portion/emor_ujafedny5761.shtml

since most Jews don't wear a kippah, they will escape at least the part about making a statement about Jews. Probably, the whole driving thing is culturally determined. In Israel, if you drove like the above-mentioned rabbi, you'd likely be considered a wimp. Jewish is as Jewish does.

The Day the Rabbi Plotzed

Speaking of rabbis, back in the 60s, Jewish author Harry Kemelman wrote a series of popular mystery novels concerning Rabbi David Small, full-time rabbi and part-time sleuth. They had titles like *Friday the Rabbi Slept Late*, *Saturday the Rabbi Went Hungry, Tuesday the Rabbi Saw Red* and so on. All in all, the rabbi seemed to have an interesting week.

Kemelman wrote several of such stories, though there was never a day of the week when Rabbi Small plotzed, or fainted away. He might well have, though, had any of his synagogue members been convicted of the various crimes that the rabbi solved through talmudic logic, all the while holding his own against conflicts with the synagogue president. In Rabbi Small's world, suspected Jews were exonerated as the rabbi honed in on the real culprit. Things were good for the Jews in Marblehead, Massachusetts, where the novels were set.

Had Kemelman been alive in recent years, though, he might well have written *Wednesday the Rabbi Plotzed.* Here's why.

In 2009, investment advisor Bernard Madoff made headlines with something more serious than bad driving. In a widely-publicized scandal, Madoff was convicted for running a huge and decades-long Ponzi scheme. By the time the story broke, some $65 billion dollars had disappeared from investors' accounts (though the actual as opposed to paper losses may have been more like $18 billion). For defrauding numerous investors, Madoff received a sentence of 150 years in prison.[4] As a well-trusted

4. "Bernard Madoff," en.wikipedia.org/wiki/Bernard_Madoff

investor and advisor, his downfall was more shocking, something like discovering that your grandmother ran numbers for the Mafia when she wasn't making stuffed cabbage.

This was bad enough for those who lost both money and trust. But Madoff was Jewish. In synagogues, JCCs and the Parsippany cousins' club, many must have been asking: "Is this going to be bad for the Jews? Why did Madoff *have* to be Jewish? Why couldn't he have been Swedish or Peruvian?"

Apart from the fact that such thinking is wishing ill on someone else—would it be better if the Swedes got a bad rap instead?—it does reflect a common reaction to discovering that an M.O.T., a Member of the Tribe, has done wrong. And so, one online commenter suggested that Orthodox Jewish organizations (the poster was Orthodox) should announce that:

> From now on, any Jew caught stealing, robbing, cheating or defrauding or creating headlines that make Jews look bad, will be BANNED from all synagogues affiliated with the OU, RCA, NCYI and Agudah [affiliations of related synagogues].

A long post followed, ending with:

> This effort would be worthwhile even if no two synagogues would agree exactly on who to ban. The important part is that our children and Gentile neighbors see us disassociate from crooks and criminals, which would help to neutralize recent Chillul HaShem by showing that Bernard Madoff and other Jewish crooks are merely diseases on the body of the Jewish people, not the body itself.[5]

5. Comment by "Nathan" in Yitzchok Adlerstein, "What's Wrong with Us?", cross-currents.com/2009/10/21/whats-wrong-with-us/

Regardless of the merits of this suggestion, the question of how Jewish behavior influences outsiders' perceptions of us is certainly not new.

At a safe chronological distance, we can now romanticize the 20th-century phenomenon of Jewish gangsters such as Meyer Lansky or Bugsy Siegel. In fact, on a trip to Las Vegas a few years ago, I visited the pink-stuccoed Flamingo Hotel, where I discovered a bronze plaque with Bugsy Siegel's face in bas-relief and an embossed biography of his life—Siegel being the former owner of the Flamingo. Mixed in with the anodyne pink architecture, the sculpted ode to a hit man was a bit surreal.

One wonders how the behavior of Jewish mobsters influenced people's perceptions of Jews in their own day. That some of them refrained from murder on Yom Kippur because it was the holiest day of the Jewish year or that they all claimed to love their mothers may not have done much to help those who felt it reflected badly on Jews that we had our "own" mob. Or maybe it *was* good for the Jews, since it showed we were not just a passive people waiting for attacks to happen.

The same question applies to the surge in Jewish boxers in the early 20th century, though there we are on safer territory than with gangsters; it's a good bet that the boxers were probably better for the Jews and the Jewish image.

Yet with more recent examples of Jews in the news—not to mention the upsurge of anti-Semitism in Europe and other parts of the world—the question of Jewish behavior becomes more serious. There is an entire website described as "a subterranean, proto-hipster workspace [where hosts Larry Rosen and Eric Goldbrener] share with you their views on topics ranging from raccoons to Middle East relations. Their show can be serious, satirical, global and mundane; no matter what the topic, it always boils down to the same question: (Is It) Good for the Jews?"[6]

6. "(Is It) Good for the Jews?" [podcast], www.isitgoodforthejews.com/about/

"Jews Gone Wild"

The idea that Jewish behavior can engender good or bad results goes back to that Jewish book of books, the Hebrew Bible. On numerous occasions, the Bible tells the Jewish people not to "profane" God's name, using the word *challel*—from which we get the phrase *chillul HaShem*. The idea is that poor behavior reflects badly not just on the Jews, but especially on the God whom Jewish people claim as their own (as in the expressions "the God of Israel" or "the God of Abraham, Isaac and Jacob"). This, it can be said, is as true of Jewish atheists as it of religious Jews—for many non-Jews the religion of Judaism is associated with all Jews just as Catholicism was with John F. Kennedy or the Sicilian mob.

The classic biblical example of chillul hashem is the incident of the Golden Calf. As a child, I would see artists' depictions of this scene on the Jewish calendars that our synagogue gave out each year. Vaguely, I recall illustrations of Jewish women dancing with tambourines and wearing flowing dresses, the scenes all taking place in front of a large gold cow. It looked something out of a Broadway musical, though the original story was a good deal darker (though not without humor).

In the original, Moses has just spent forty days and nights on Mount Sinai, where he received the Ten Commandments on tablets of stone, written "with the finger of God."[7] In this tale, patience is not one of Israel's outstanding qualities and patience finally runs out waiting for Moses to return. Admittedly, if someone went on an errand and didn't return for a month plus, you might start wondering what happened to them too. As it turns out, Israel does more than just wonder.

The people run amok, crying out that they have no idea what happened to Moses, so let's make some gods of our own

7. Exodus 31:18.

to worship. You would think, *taka*,[8] that they would send out a search party. But instead they remove their jewelry and melt it down into an idol—the infamous Golden Calf. After sacrificing to the idol, in the biblical wording, "they sat down to eat and drink, and then rose to dance."[9] They were not doing the *hora*; what this really implies is revelry. In other words, what we have is not very flattering: Jews gone wild.

Clearly, someone had to be a skillful artisan to make a calf sculpted out of gold. Nevertheless, in what is likely the lamest excuse in all history, Moses' brother Aaron explains to the infuriated Moses, who has finally arrived on the scene, that "… I said to them, 'Whoever has gold, take it off!' They gave it to me and I hurled it into the fire and out came this calf!"[10] At this point we must wonder if any non-Jews watching would have faulted Israel's ethics or their intelligence—or again, admired their ability to make excuses. Sometimes you just can't tell what will be good or bad for the Jews.

In the case of the Golden Calf, the Bible definitely sides with "bad for the Jews," and bad for what non-Jews will end up thinking about the God that these Jews profess to worship. The Bible frequently warns against behavior that reflects poorly on Jews and in turn poorly on God. "You shall not profane My holy name, that I may be sanctified in the midst of the Israelite people—I the LORD who sanctify you …" the Torah says.[11]

It falls to the prophet Ezekiel to make the special point that when God's people behave badly, it affects God's "reputation" among non-Jews: "I will sanctify My great name which has been profaned among the nations—among whom you have caused it to be profaned. And the nations shall know that I am the LORD—

8. Yiddish for "really," with the implication, "Wouldn't you really think that…?"

9. Exodus 32:6.

10. Exodus 32:24.

11. Lev. 22:32; you can also have a look at Lev. 18:21; Ps. 74:7; Is. 48:11; Jer. 34:16; Ezek. 20:9, Amos 2:7.

declares the Lord GOD—when I manifest My holiness before their eyes through you."[12] This is one of many biblical examples where, when Jews pull a Bernie Madoff and fail to sanctify God's name—when they do a chillul haShem instead of a kiddush haShem—God pulls out his online reputation management software[13] and sanctifies His own name. That is, he acts in a way that restores and enhances his name and character. Presumably if he didn't do it, no one else would.

But the ideal for the Jewish people is the opposite: to live up to their calling, to perform acts of kiddush haShem. Not only will such acts reflect well on Jews, but in turn, the Bible tells us, it will reflect well on God with whom we are associated. It's the Bible's version of walk the walk, don't just talk the talk.

When the *Goyim* Did Kiddush (and Chillul) haShem

The Jewish value of kiddush haShem continued beyond the Hebrew Bible. In the New Testament, examples of this value are addressed to both Jewish and Gentile followers of Jesus.

Clearly, the importance of behavior that is kiddush haShem was on Jesus' mind. Do a kiddush haShem and it reflects not just on you, but on the God you claim to be following:

> "… let your light shine before people, so that they may see the good things you do and praise your Father in heaven."[14]

Similarly, Peter wrote to followers of Jesus living in the diaspora regions:

> … live such good lives among the pagans that even though they now speak against you as evil-doers, they will, as a result of seeing your good actions, give glory to God on the Day of his coming.[15]

12. Ezek. 36:23.
13. See, e.g., support.google.com/accounts/answer/1228138?hl=en?rel=
14. Matt. 5:16.
15. 1 Peter 2:12.

Another translation gives the final phrase as "glorify God on the day he visits us."[16] When I lived in Brooklyn, I used to visit my cousins in New Jersey all the time for barbeque or just to hang out. When God "visits," it's not to hang out or have grilled hamburgers, but refers to the time when he will come and set all injustices aright. Before that day arrives, though, there was daily reality to deal with. This, according to Peter, included non-Jews doing chillul haShem: slandering "as evil-doers" the Jewish people and even other non-Jews who had joined in following Jesus (a move which at that time was considered to be joining a Jewish group).

Some of those anti-Semitic charges were that Jews undermined the public good and acted contrary to proper civic values. And of course, this would mean that the religion of Judaism (of which faith in Jesus was a sub-set in the first century) and the God of the Jews were also engaged in social malfeasance. And so, after the above-quoted exhortation, Peter gives a whole section on ethical behavior designed to counter the slanders and in turn reflect well, not only on the Jews but on the God of the Jews.[17]

Paul also has something to say. In his Letter to the Romans, he sets up what he sees as humanity's core problem and how to address that problem. The problem according to Paul is that *everyone*, Jewish or Gentile, is engaged in chillul haShem. Put another way, everyone sins, something which we acknowledge every Yom Kippur. Everyone acts in a way that reflects poorly not only on themselves but, if they profess faith in God, on the God they claim to believe in.

---

16. New International Version.

17. See Craig S. Keener, *The IVP Bible Background Commentary: New Testament* (Downers Grove, IL: InterVarsity Press, 1993) on 1 Peter 2:12: "Jewish people living in the Diaspora (1:1) always had to be concerned about Gentiles' anti-Jewish slanders, for their safety and for their witness to the one true God. Just as Gentiles were more than happy to slander Jews living among them, they were happy to slander Gentile converts to what they viewed as a Jewish sect, Christianity (2:4-10). The behavior advocated in the following household codes (2:13–3:12) would undermine some of the most traditional slanders against such faiths, slanders that they subverted the public order and traditional family values."

Paul's readership—or perhaps listenership, as oral reading of letters to congregations was common, sort of a first-century podcast—was a congregation in Rome that was a mix of Jews and non-Jews. In his letter, Paul first addresses non-Jews, reminding them that they fall short of their own ethical ideals by their behavior. Then he addresses his fellow Jews, who have the Bible to guide them yet also engage in chillul haShem.

> . . . you who teach others, don't you teach yourself? Preaching, **"Thou shalt not steal,"** do you steal? Saying, **"Thou shalt not commit adultery,"** do you commit adultery? Detesting idols, do you commit idolatrous acts? You who take such pride in *Torah*, do you, by disobeying the *Torah*, dishonor God?—as it says in the *Tanakh*, **"For it is because of you that God's name is blasphemed by the *Goyim*."**[18]

At this point in time, the only place these things were said was the Hebrew Bible; the New Testament had not yet come into existence. Paul is quoting from Ezekiel 36:23 to make the point that while the behavior of non-Jews falls short of their own ideals, the behavior of Jews can reflect poorly on the Jews and on God as well. Non-Jews do not live up to their consciences and Jews do not live up to the Scriptures. (All this is Paul's set up to presenting his solution to the problem of universal chillul haShem—see chapter 8.)

Jesus the Martyr?

At some point in Jewish history, the term "kiddush haShem" became associated with more than just acts of kindness and justice; it began to be used specifically for martyrdom. When confronted in medieval times with the choice of forced conversion to Christianity (usually Catholicism) or death, many Jews chose the latter—and died, according to reports, reciting the words of

18. Romans 2:21-24. Boldface original.

the *Shema*. This was considered the ultimate act of sanctifying God's name, by remaining loyal to the God of Israel. Here there was no question of whether the act of martyrdom was good or bad for the Jews—it was simply laying down one's life in service to God, performing the ultimate sacrifice. But since this kind of faithfulness undoubtedly strengthened the faith of other Jews and helped ensure the survival, rather than the assimilation of the Jewish people, we can judge it good for the Jews as well.

A martyr need not be someone who chooses death over conversion. As the word is variously used, it can mean someone who is killed for their beliefs or killed simply because of who they are. It can refer to someone who gives up their life in the cause of a movement or purpose.

Take a poll of Jewish people and pose the question, "Who was Jesus?" At one time, the answer would not have been very flattering, but it is now common to hear that he was a rabbi, or a good teacher, or the first Reform Jew (in other words, he upset the religious apple cart), or a prophet, or a martyr. What many have in mind by the last description is that Jesus died at the hands of Rome, perishing in a Messianic cause that didn't pan out.

As it happens, there is a large assortment of modern Jewish writers and poets who have written about Jesus's death as martyrdom, firmly placing Jesus within his Jewish milieu alongside the multitude of other Jews who died martyrs' deaths. Matthew Hoffman writes that "for almost all modern Jewish writers Jesus' death is understood more within the Jewish tradition of martyrdom than the Christian tradition of vicarious atonement and sacrifice."[19]

I think viewing Jesus' death as that of a martyr dying for a purpose, or a cause, can be helpful. The New Testament, however, does not picture the death of Jesus as that of a victim overrun by powerful

19. Matthew Hoffman, *From Rebel to Rabbi: Reclaiming Jesus and the Making of Modern Jewish Culture* (Stanford, Stanford University Press, 2007), p. 125.

external forces. In contrast to the Jews of later centuries who were murdered by no choice of their own, the New Testament portrays Jesus as willingly going to his death in service to his "cause." (Some medieval Jews also willingly went to their death rather than choose a forced conversion, but read on.) Jesus' own words were:

> "I am the good shepherd. The good shepherd lays down his life for the sheep."[20]

The idea behind the metaphor is not that sheep are mindless followers, but that they are vulnerable and need a shepherd to steer and guide them. The idea is foreign to modern urbanites—the wildest animal I ever saw growing up in Brooklyn was a pigeon—but sheep are frequent biblical images for people in need of protection, guidance and care, all of which was provided by the ancient occupation of shepherd.

A good shepherd, as opposed to a lazy one, guarded the flock against predatory animals as well as thieves who would have loved to seize some of the flock for a lamb chop dinner. A shepherd was like a Boy Scout troop leader and security guard rolled into one. Would this guard be slacking off, checking his iPhone or napping? Or would he be vigilant, if need be even sacrificing his own life for the sake of keeping the flock safe—in other words, a good shepherd?

> ... I lay down my life—in order to take it up again! No one takes it away from me; on the contrary, I lay it down of my own free will. …[21]

Here, just a few verses after the first quote, we find Jesus stating the same thing in even starker terms, along with the implication that he will be raised from the dead ("in order to take it up again").

20. John 10:11.
21. John 10:17-18.

Paul continues this line of thought when he writes of the voluntary nature of Jesus' death and its purpose. That there *was* a purpose may be an odd conception. Someone reportedly was asked, "Why did Jesus die?" and their very reasonable response was, "Because he stopped breathing." Beyond the medical description of death, however, there was an underlying reason that Jesus gave up his own life, as Paul explains:

> For while we were still helpless, at the right time, the Messiah died on behalf of ungodly people. Now it is a rare event when someone gives up his life even for the sake of somebody righteous, although possibly for a truly good person one might have the courage to die. But God demonstrates his own love for us in that the Messiah died on our behalf while we were still sinners.[22]

According to Paul and other New Testament writers, the purpose of Jesus' death was to atone for our sins. Paul invokes common human behavior: most people do not willingly give up their lives for another person. Someone might sacrifice themselves in battle to save a buddy, or to get someone else out of harm's way. But that is not typical behavior; the media have even reported on times when crowds have stood around observing a crime in action without doing anything to stop it, the so-called "Bystander Effect."[23] Much less do people choose self-sacrifice for someone they consider enemies. But Jesus, says Paul, gave up his own life even while humanity stood opposed to God.

Now *that* is a kiddush haShem!

22. Romans 5:6-8.

23. See, e.g., "Defining the Bystander Effect: Kitty Genovese Murder & Research by Latane and Darley," study.com/academy/lesson/defining-the-bystander-effect-kitty-genovese-murder-research-by-latane-and-darley.html

So, Is It Good for the Jews?

Jesus' death as a kiddush haShem is portrayed in the New Testament as very good for the Jews, indeed. When Jesus was brought by his parents to Jerusalem for his consecration (the first-century version of today's pidyon ha-ben ceremony), an old man named Simeon (or Shimon) was hanging around. Apparently, he was also a poet (artistic types always seem to be hanging around), because when he saw Jesus and his parents,

> Shim'on took him in his arms, made a *b'rakhah* to God, and said,
> "Now, ADONAI, according to your word,
> your servant is at peace as you let him go;
> for I have seen with my own eyes your *yeshu'ah* [salvation],
> which you prepared in the presence of all peoples—
> a light that will bring revelation to the *Goyim*
> and *glory to your people Isra'el.*"[24]

Whatever the exact implication of "glory to your people Israel" entailed, it was certainly something good for the Jews. And there can never be enough of that in the world!

24. Luke 2:28-32; emphasis in final phrase added.

CHAPTER 4

WHEN SPEECH GOES SOUTH

(Lashon Hara)

You may need a break from this book at this point, so here's an activity to stretch your limbs with. Open up a feather pillow, go outside and throw the contents everywhere you can. Let the wind take the feathers or let them just fall to the ground. Let the cars in the street roll over them. Bonus points if some birds come and take them away. Maybe some passersby will stop to pick a few up, just because they can.

Now comes the fun part. Collect all the feathers and stuff them back into the pillow. Preferably get this done before the person who uses the pillow notices that it's gone.

Not easy and probably impossible, right? The scenario is based on an old rabbinic story that talks about the effects of gossip and malicious talk. Like the feathers, the rabbis pointed out, once out of our mouths, our words go everywhere. They can be picked up by others as they are carried along and re-spoken, but they cannot be unspoken.[1] In Jewish thinking, what happens in Vegas does *not* stay in Vegas. That was true enough centuries ago; if the rabbis of the Talmud were suddenly brought to our age of social media, they would undoubtedly have, in the words of my mother, a conniption.

Lashon hara, it is called in Jewish tradition. Literally this means "an evil tongue" or "evil speech." It's more than just idle

1. Telushkin, *Jewish Literacy*, pp. 522-23.

chatter about someone. It embraces hate speech, perjury before a grand jury, lying about your late-night affair with the blonde at the office and deliberately sowing mistrust among colleagues as you seek to rise in the hierarchy. It includes politicians smearing their colleagues as well as Steve Jobs' infamous way of reportedly meandering down cubicles and goading employees with lines like, "Brian in the next office … his work sucks, doesn't it?"[2]

Truth be told, there is a certain fondness for lesser forms of lashon hara such as the gossip that occurs within a close-knit community (whether any forms are truly lesser, I will leave to the philosophers). The yenta is a fondly-remembered classic character in Jewish literature and life. The word "yenta," now widely used in English, is defined variously as a busybody, meddler, or gossip. The venerable *Merriam-Webster Dictionary* offers this slightly disturbing example of how to use the word: "The couple's loud quarrel had the building's *yentas* yapping for a week."[3] Due to the popularity of *Fiddler on the Roof*, where Yente was the name of the matchmaker, it is sometimes used in that connection as well.[4] (And Molly Picon's performance undoubtedly contributed to the grandmotherly, innocent image of the neighborhood yenta.) So, we find the mobile phone app Yenta that "connects Jewish singles with other singles near them!"[5] And don't even ask about Rent-A-Yenta, which is, inexplicably, a housecleaning service.[6] Presumably after cleaning homes in a given neighborhood, the employees will have plenty to dish about.

---

2. Technically, *lashon hara* is one specific kind of evil speech, namely gossip, there being other names that refer to other varieties. For simplicity I'm using the phrase to cover all kinds of evil, malicious, or hurtful speech.

3. "Yenta," www.merriam-webster.com/dictionary/yenta

4. The word's origins, though, precede the Broadway musical by many centuries. It, and the related name Yentl, may have originated from the Romance-language *gentile* (which would be pronounced *jen-teel-a*), meaning "noble, refined." See, e.g., "Yentl," www.avotaynu.com/books/yentl.htm

5. "Free Yenta iPhone App Finds Jewish Dates by Location," www.jewishhumorcentral.com/2012/10/free-yenta-iphone-app-finds-jewish.html

6. "Rent-A-Yenta House Cleaning Service," www.facebook.com/Rent-A-Yenta-House-Cleaning-Service-136821933033118/

Of course, not all "evil speech" is grandmotherly. In 2014, the Anne Frank Center USA held an art exhibit titled, "Lashon Hara: On the Consequences of Hate Speech." It presented the work of textile artist Robin Atlas and was advertised as intending to show the physical as well as spiritual consequences of evil speech. As the press release put it:

> Words have always been a catalyst for destruction, but today hate speech is increasingly prevalent—tearing apart the fabric of our communities in ever more violent and destructive ways. Around the world, religious hostilities are at a six year high. While in America alone, the number of hate groups has increased by 56 percent since 2000.[7]

On another note related to lashon hara, *Tablet* Magazine noted the longstanding correspondence between lyricist and composer Stephen Sondheim and his late friend Arthur Laurents.[8] Sondheim's lawyer had "written a letter threatening legal action if any of his correspondence is published and who, in a very reasonable sounding email to the *New York Post's* theater columnist Michael Riedel, cited a concern for hurting the feelings of friends and colleagues about whom he may have engaged in gossip some 40 years ago." *Tablet* then opined, "Look, it's impossible not to gossip—it's how we bond with others. What's possible is to try to spare the feelings of your subjects. So along with … every other accolade Sondheim has accrued over his lengthy and distinguished career, we offer him one more: rabbi."

Spice Merchants and Slithering

Tablet's disclaimer aside, avoidance of gossip, slander and lying are Jewish (though not exclusively Jewish) values. And for

7. Figures as of 2014, "The Anne Frank Center USA Proudly Presents 'Lashon Hara: On the Consequences of Hate Speech'," www.prweb.com/releases/2014/11/prweb12336281.htm
8. Rachel Shukert, "Rabbi Stephen Sondheim," www.tabletmag.com/scroll/169206/rabbi-stephen-sondheim

Jews, the origin is once again to be found in the Hebrew Bible. For example:

> Do not deal basely with your countrymen. Do not profit by the blood of your fellow: I am the LORD.[9]

Here, "do not deal basely" more literally means something like "don't go around as a slanderer." The verse uses the Hebrew word *rakhil*, which comes from a term for a travelling spice merchant. Apparently, some merchants enjoyed spicing up more than just their food and picked up juicy gossip as they went along. Or maybe the idea was that gossip travels far and wide like a merchant who covers the globe.

The phrase "profit by the blood of your fellow" in the same verse refers in context to a capital court case; false testimony and perjury are in view. Don't be like a travelling salesman, spreading lies that can land someone in court. (If any upstanding travelling salespeople still exist who are reading this, my apologies to you.)

> Who is the man who is eager for life,
> who desires years of good fortune?
> Guard your tongue from evil,
> your lips from deceitful speech.[10]

Though the phrase "lashon hara" is not actually found in any of these biblical passages (it is a later umbrella term that covers many kinds of speech that have gone south), Psalm 34 does say to "guard your tongue from evil," using the same Hebrew words *lashon* ("tongue") and *ra* ("evil"). The context of this psalm, by the way, is given in its title, "when he [David] feigned madness in the presence of Abimelech, who turned him out, and he left."

The background is that the first king Israel ever had, Saul, felt threatened by David's increasing popularity to the point that David had to flee for his life. David accordingly fled from the frying

9. Leviticus 19:16.
10. Psalm 34:13-14. Verses 12-13 in other English translations.

pan into the fire, ending up with the Philistine king of Gath.[11] Not a good choice. To get away from the king of Gath, David starred in his own production of *The Mad King*: he "concealed his good sense from them; he feigned madness for their benefit. He scratched marks on the doors of the gate and let his saliva run down his beard."[12] I guess if someone acted like that around me, I'd send them away too. It's not clear if this verse from the psalm's warning about an evil tongue is intended for people like Saul who indeed told lies about David or is David's own reflection that perhaps deceptive theatrics don't accomplish as much as living the right kind of life.

> He who conceals hatred has lying lips,
> While he who speaks forth slander is a dullard.[13]

Here we have yet another image: "slander" here is a bad "report" (*dibbah*). According to some, "speak forth" is better rendered as "spreading" slander and is possibly related to something meaning to move slowly or glide along, not a bad description of how gossip can slither person to person before completing its mischief, like a game of "Telephone" gone awry. The JPS *Tanakh*'s "dullard" is more often translated "fool," who biblically speaking is someone who can't manage their own life properly—part of which is common sense and much of which involves trusting God. In this case, being a conduit for lashon hara is an indication that someone hasn't learned some basic life lessons.

Lies, Damn Lies and __

Modern Western law has provisions for slander and libel. In some European countries, Holocaust denial is almost a form of lashon hara, though of course not called by that name. But those

11. Given as "Achish" in 1 Samuel 21:10 and as "Abimelech" in Psalm 34. Achish would have been his name; Abimelech was a title, like Pharaoh.
12. 1 Samuel 21:14. Verse 13 in other English translations.
13. Proverbs 10:18.

laws make the point that denying the Holocaust is a form of lying that has social consequences.

Jewish tradition gives us many examples of the consequences of "evil speech." Moses' sister Miriam was afflicted with leprosy by God for slandering her brother. The Talmud and the Midrash say[14] that the cause of the destruction of the Temple in 70 C.E. was the moral condition of that generation—specifically, Jews slandering their fellow Jews. The serpent in the Garden of Eden spoke evil of God to Eve, who listened and believed the serpent's evil speech (listening to and believing lashon hara are forbidden in Jewish thinking as much as speaking it). The consequences for Eve were getting herself and her equally complicit husband kicked out of Eden and bringing ruination down on all of humanity. Clearly, for the rabbi's words can carry the power of a destructive tsunami. Some went as far as to compare lashon hara with murder.[15]

Just when you thought the water was safe, tradition goes even further: people are forbidden from speaking negatively about someone else, even if the information is true. (I know of few people who abide by this principle, least of all in the arenas of politics and tabloid journalism.) Tradition is not rigid; there are exceptions when one really needs to provide such information, such as when a prospective employer needs to know about the applicants, or in cases of abuse.[16]

If you go to services on Yom Kippur, you will probably recite a prayer called *Al Chet*, which means "For the sin." In this lengthy prayer, we ask for forgiveness for things we did that we shouldn't have done and for things we didn't do that we should have done. It

---

14. *b. Gittin* 55b; *Deuteronomy Rabbah* 6:14. See www.dinonline.org/wp-content/uploads/newsletter/en_106.pdf: "The Midrash (Devarim Rabba 6:14) writes that *lashon hara* was even the cause of the destruction of the Temple: 'On account of the *lashon hara* among them, I have removed My Shechinah from among them.' This is reflected in the Talmudic teaching whereby the Second Temple was destroyed on account of baseless hatred, as embodied in the tragic tale of Kamtza and bar Kamtza (*Gittin* 55b)."

15. *b. Arakhin* 15b: "The School of R. Ishmael taught: Whoever speaks slander increases his sins even up to [the degree of] the three [cardinal] sins: idolatry, incest, and the shedding of blood" (Soncino edition).

16. For the general principle, see Telushkin, *Jewish Literacy*, p. 523.

turns out that 43 sins are mentioned, of which 11 have to do with sins of our speech.[17]

If most modern Jews don't go as far as avoiding all negative comments about others, much less equating such talk with murder, still we disapprove of gossip, slander and lying—even if we engage in those activities ourselves. This may partly explain the market for "No Lashon Hara" T-shirts, mugs and caps,[18] another part being that some might find it to be a fashion statement of Jewish cool. Jews like to be reminded of our ideals, even when we fall short.

The curious reader might wonder why the power of *positive* speech does not seem to get as much attention. True, the book of Proverbs does mention "sweet," "pleasing," "excellent," and "gracious" speech.[19] Everyone knows that uplifting, encouraging words can make a young child confident and well-adjusted; can bring cheer to a shut-in; can inspire a generation. So why all the attention focused on negative and hurtful words? My guess is that as with many things in life, we often need to root out the negative to encourage the positive. Healing a disease takes precedence over encouraging a patient in their exercise program. Take care of what's negative, and in many cases the positive will follow.

Horses, Sea Cruises and the Zoo

As a Jewish book, the New Testament is no stranger to the power of speech. The book of James[20] offers a perspective on speech. "Anyone who thinks he is religiously observant," writes James, "but does not control his tongue is deceiving himself, and

17. Liel Leibovitz, "'Lashon Hara': Available Now on a Phone Near You," www.tabletmag.com/jewish-arts-and-culture/162932/lashon-hara-secret-app

18. E.g., "Black and White No Lashon Hara Graphic T-Shirt," www.zazzle.com/black_and_white_no_lashon_hara_graphic_t_shirt-235649431772680225

19. Proverbs 16:21, 17:7, 22:11. The exact words vary depending on the translation.

20. There are several "Jameses" in the New Testament and the letter does not specify which of these is the author, or whether it is another James altogether. A number of scholars argue for James the brother of Jesus as the writer. But the book itself doesn't "give away the goods."

his observance counts for nothing."[21] For James, words are like a horse that can gallop away at any moment. He would clearly have little patience for someone who says, "I go to shul every Friday night," and then lets loose with gossip. In fact, James immediately goes on to say that worthwhile "religious observance" includes caring for orphans and widows.[22] In other words, if you have nothing worthwhile to say, don't just say nothing—*do* something positive.

Later in his book, James returns to the topic, waxing eloquent on the subject.

> For we all stumble in many ways; if someone does not stumble in what he says, he is a mature man who can bridle his whole body. If we put a bit into a horse's mouth to make it obey us, we control its whole body as well.[23]

James often sounds a lot like the book of Proverbs. Like a fine wine, a good proverb is meant to be smelled, inhaled, kept on the tongue a while, mulled over, swallowed and its finish to be enjoyed. When it comes to biblical proverbs, letting their meanings and connotations swirl through our minds slowly helps us appreciate and apply them. Here James invites us to do just that with his own proverbial writing.

And so we swirl and taste what he means by "controlling" our mouths, which in the underlying Greek also suggests "keeping a rein on." As we reflect on it, it seems it is more than just making like cookware by putting a lid on it. If you have ever ridden a horse, or been in a horse-drawn carriage, you realize that pulling the reins isn't just for stopping. It's also for turning, adjusting, getting the horse ready to move in another direction. In other words, it can be the prelude to more activity.

21. James 1:26.
22. See chapter 6.
23. James 3:2-3.

Refusing to engage in negative speech, or stopping it before it comes out, allows us to engage in positive things. No wonder that James contrasts evil speech with caring for widows and orphans. Avoiding gossip, slander and lying frees one up from having to deal with negative consequences and allows us the time, energy and strength of character to impact the world around us in positive ways.

> And think of a ship—although it is huge and is driven by strong winds, yet the pilot can steer it wherever he wants with just a small rudder.[24]

James nuances the point here with his nautical metaphor. James is an equal opportunity metaphor-maker. If you're not familiar with horses, maybe you've been on a cruise and can relate to a different picture. Here the point is similar to the rein image—both reins and rudders steer—but James amplifies it. The tiny rudder has enormous power to move a huge, storm-buffeted ship. Swirling this image around like fine wine, we may contemplate how the tiny tongue can move people, institutions, even history in a way out of all proportion to its physical size. "I have a dream," said Martin Luther King. "That means war!" pronounces a dictator.

> So too the tongue is a tiny part of the body, yet it boasts great things. See how a little fire sets a whole forest ablaze! Yes, the tongue is a fire, a world of wickedness. The tongue is so placed in our body that it defiles every part of it, setting ablaze the whole of our life; and it is set on fire by Gei-Hinnom [hell] itself.[25]

For those whose experience includes neither horses nor houseboats, here James addresses the weekend campers in their RVs. In California where I am writing, the news reports during the dry

---

24. James 3:4.
25. James 3:5-6.

season invariably include accounts of fires, often near populated areas, brought about by high winds or arson. At that time of year, wooded areas can be tinderboxes and it does not take much for a fire to begin. Here James gets more direct and away from the "swirl my words" typical of proverbs. The tongue, he says, is a "world of evil" among all our bodily parts. It can corrupt us and ruin our lives. And anyone who doubts that hell has anything to do with evil speech might think twice after considering what Hitler's words did to a generation of Germans.

> For people have tamed and continue to tame all kinds of animals, birds, reptiles and sea creatures; but the tongue no one can tame—it is an unstable and evil thing, full of death-dealing poison! [26]

This time we're off to the zoo to see the birdhouse, the snake house and the fish tank. Unfortunately, while there are signs reading THIS WAY TO THE LIONS, THIS WAY TO THE PENGUINS,[27] there is no cage where we can view The Human Tongue, detached from its habitat and subject to the feeding schedule of the zookeeper. Like an ever-prowling venomous animal, it remains "in the wild," never to be captured, never to be exhibited before admiring, admission-paying crowds.

Much of this may come across as a bit overwrought to modern readers. But it makes its point. Whether we are Orthodox Jews parsing finely the different kinds of negative speech, or secular haven't-been-to-synagogue-since-my-bar-mitzvah Jews, most people recognize that speaking ill of others is not an admirable virtue, even if we engage in it. Try this experiment: the next time you write a list of New Year's resolutions, see if "I want to be a

26. James 3:7-8.

27. P.T. Barnum reportedly got crowds to exit his zoo quickly in order to make room for a fresh batch of paying customers. He is said to have posted signs TO THE LIONESS, TO THE TIGRESS and TO THE EGRESS. Eager to see the egress, customers headed out the exit door before learning that "egress" means "the way out."

better, more eloquent gossip and liar this year" ends up on your list alongside exercising more, being nicer to that obnoxious cousin and giving more back to society.

> With it [the tongue] we bless *ADONAI*, the Father; and with it we curse people, who were made **in the image of God**. Out of the same mouth come blessing and cursing! Brothers, it isn't right for things to be this way. A spring doesn't send both fresh and bitter water from the same opening, does it? Can a fig tree yield olives, my brothers? or a grapevine, figs? Neither does salt water produce fresh.[28]

Farmers and naturalists—you are now on deck. I know next to nothing about farming and next to next to nothing about nature; growing up in New York City, I'm not sure we even had an outside. But about an hour and a half drive east of where I now live near San Francisco, you enter the world of almond trees, orange groves and olives. Head south for some forty-five minutes and you encounter Gilroy, the self-proclaimed "Garlic Capital of the World." Even an urbanite knows that almond growers don't sell pomegranates. Gilroy will not suddenly turn into the Kumquat Capital. As far as salt vs. fresh water goes, bottled water is advertised as "From Mountain Springs," not "From the Bottom of the Sea." Each kind produces its own.

Yet, says James, there is a real problem. Or as my New Jersey friends used to say: "We got a situation here." The conundrum is that in every other sphere of nature that we see, like produces like. Yet our tongues can praise God and simultaneously slander another human being who is in the very likeness of the same God we just praised. Something is unique about the behavior of human beings and James recognizes that.

---

28. James 3:9-12. Boldface original.

Brain-Dead Dummies of Judea

While James gets the award for the most variety of images in the New Testament that depict lashon hara, it was probably some of Jesus' own sayings that sparked James' creative metaphor-making.

One of the most memorable sections of the New Testament is known as the Sermon on the Mount. Whereas in my synagogue growing up, the sermon was the occasion for many to step outside and have a smoke (after all, they already knew what the rabbi thought about things!), people seemed to gravitate to hear Jesus speak. The Sermon on the Mount is really about ethics, the ethics of the "Kingdom of God," an ethic almost unlivable in the present world. But Jesus uses extremes of language to drive home his points.

Here are Jesus' own remarks:

> "You have heard that our fathers were told, **'Do not murder,'** and that anyone who commits murder will be subject to judgment. But I tell you that anyone who nurses anger against his brother will be subject to judgment; that whoever calls his brother, 'You good-for-nothing!' will be brought before the *Sanhedrin*; that whoever says, 'Fool!' incurs the penalty of burning in the fire of Gei-Hinnom [hell]![29]

In his words on lashon hara, Jesus stands in agreement with other Jewish thinkers on the seriousness of words and the inner thoughts that precede them. Some decades after Jesus, the New Testament author John writes that "everyone who hates his brother is a murderer."[30] Eliezer ben Hyrcanus, around 100 C.E., maintained that, "One who hates his neighbor is among those who shed blood."[31] The Talmud, several centuries after Jesus, considered

---

29. Matthew 5:21-22. Boldface original.
30. 1 John 3:15.
31. Cited in R. T. France, *The Gospel of Matthew* (Grand Rapids, MI/Cambridge, UK, 2007), p. 199, citing *Derekh Eretz Rabbah* 57b (11:13).

that "He who publicly shames his neighbour is as though he shed blood."[32] Strong words, indeed.

By the way, when Jesus says, "You have heard … but I tell you," he is not contradicting the Torah. Had he been referring to the Torah, he would have said, "It is written," not "You have heard that it was said." Rather, he was referring to popular understandings of the Torah, the way it was understood and applied, the way people learned it from their parents and teachers, the way it was repeated at the watering trough and the back alleys and the shoemaker's shop. Sometimes that was the same as what the Torah had to say; sometimes not.

So, Jesus begins by citing the commandment against murdering. That's clear enough: murder is a bad thing and carries consequences. But wait, says Jesus, there's more. Anger carries the same consequences as well and Jesus' following words show that the anger is one that is expressed verbally. This is not the justified anger whose target is injustice or poverty or a child's reckless behavior. Jesus himself became angry on occasion. This anger is destructive, not constructive. *Raca* was a word in the everyday language of Aramaic, meaning *empty*. Calling someone *raca* was calling them empty-headed, one light bulb short of a circuit, one clown short of a circus.

"You fool"—"Idiot! Moron!"—meant about the same thing. Or even more, for in the book of Proverbs, a "fool" is one who ignores the way God designed the universe, forgets how human interactions should work, fails to see that acts produce consequences and in the process makes a wreck of his or her life. In that sense, calling someone a *fool* is telling them that they can't get their act together in life. In the culture of the time, when shame and honor meant a great deal, such a shaming epithet would carry more weight than it does today.

---

32. *b. Baba Metzia* 58b, Soncino edition; see also *b. Arakhin* 15b, referenced above. This is just the tip of the iceberg as far as rabbinic comments about evil speech go.

And those expressions must have been commonly used, or else there would be no point to Jesus' using them as examples. Were the streets of Judea filled with disgruntled people shouting, "You brain-dead dummy!"? Perhaps. Today's sports stadiums resound with similar sentiments. And judging from the uncivil tone of many social media "conversations," there are a lot of people who would like to give others a piece of their mind and then some. When people voice their disagreement on message boards with, "Why don't you crawl back into the hole you came from!" they are not acting much differently than those who said *raca!* and *fool!*

In Jesus' scenario, three punishments are meted out for these offenses. They are likely different ways of expressing the same thing, namely, that we're talking about serious behavior which carries serious consequences. Perhaps there is even an escalation from one punishment to the next.

First Jesus mentions that anger, like murder, renders a person "subject to judgment." If he meant judgment in a court of law, that would have been an attention-getting device, for anger is hardly prosecutable. Perhaps a smile came to the lips of Jesus' listeners.

Or he could have been referring to God's future day of judgment. To many people, that must have seemed far off, something that would happen someday but nothing that would really impact their life right now. Perhaps their familiarity, or overfamiliarity with the Bible, which spoke often of that coming day of judgment (using the expression "the Day of the Lord"), led to a kind of dullness of the "Been there, done that" variety. A future judgment may have seemed like the way growing old appears to a 19-year-old: I know I'll be forty someday, but it won't be in *my* lifetime.

The second punishment involved coming before the Sanhedrin, the Supreme Court of ancient Israel which consisted of 70 individuals, not merely nine like the American system. Again, it could be that Jesus is suggesting that anger is a triable offense and again, listeners would have paid attention to such an offbeat idea. After all, given the common human penchant for calling people names, putting people on trial for getting angry—or for thinking angry thoughts—would have effectively tied up the Jerusalem court system for the foreseeable future.

Just like the first punishment of "judgment," this could alternately refer to a future divine reckoning, Jesus may even be referring to a heavenly Sanhedrin, said in Jewish tradition to be the counterpart to the human Sanhedrin. If God's future day of judgment didn't motivate people, perhaps facing 70 Judge Judys in the future life would. (We'll leave to one side for now Judge Judy's own penchant for calling people "idiots," which in light of Jesus' words would mean the good judge would end up facing 70 of herself.)

And then comes the third punishment, the rather shocking mention of "Gei-Hinnom" or hell. As commentator R. T. France remarks, "The totally unexpected conclusion in 'hellfire' comes as a shocking jolt to the complacency of the hearer, who might well have chuckled over the incongruous image of a person being tried for anger or for conventional insult, only to be pulled up short by the saying's conclusion."[33]

This is the language of shock, the jarring commercial that interrupts the TV show, an agitprop maneuver to get people to take seriously the fact that "just because everyone does it" doesn't make it right. Certainly, Jesus and the Jews of his day believed in an afterlife in which final justice would be meted out. Nevertheless, if a single "You moron!" meant that the curtain fell, the play was over and the theater went dark, no one would get off the hook. But along with the belief in the afterlife came the knowledge that forgiveness was available to those who transgressed in these areas such as speech, as Jesus emphasizes elsewhere:

---

33. France, *Gospel of Matthew*, p. 201.

> "Watch yourselves! If your brother sins, rebuke him; and if he repents, forgive him. Also, if seven times in one day he sins against you, and seven times he comes to you and says, 'I repent,' you are to forgive him."[34]

Language like this is meant to make people wake up and smell the coffee. Verbal anger, inward or outward, can lead to murder or otherwise inflict serious damage. We can probably all think of situations where uncalled for anger led to destructive consequences and made us long for a heavenly tribunal to step in to bring judgment and justice.

"Sticks and stones can break my bones," some of us learned as children, "but words can never harm me." As it turns out, words can be worse than sticks and stones. No wonder the New Testament writer Paul told his congregation of Jesus-followers, "Get rid of all bitterness, rage, anger, violent assertiveness and slander, along with all spitefulness."[35]

Some years ago, Rabbi Moshe Soloway advertised "The Evil Tongue Workshop" in conjunction with the Russian American Jewish Experience. The ad is almost impossible to find any more on Google,[36] but it featured a rather scary looking purple mouth with a tongue covered with small but sharp spikes. "Fact," the poster announced, complete with yellow triangular warning sign. "Gossip kills. Fact. Gossip destroys relationships." Learn about lashon hara, the ad urged. "It might save a life!"

Jesus would have agreed.

---

34. Luke 17:3-4.
35. Ephesians 4:31.
36. A thumbnail version can be seen at www.rajeusa.com/right_menu3.php

CHAPTER 5

HOSPITALITY

(Hakhnasat Orchim)

Growing up in New York City, I and countless other schoolchildren were familiar with the Statue of Liberty—almost as familiar as we were with our own family. For all I knew, Lady Liberty could have been modeled on a second cousin twice removed. Sometime during grade school, I was introduced to Emma Lazarus' poem, "The New Colossus." Her sonnet, concerning immigration, had been inscribed on a plaque at the Statue some twenty years after its original composition. Probably the most well-known part of Lazarus' poem is the following. It has been set to music, using a tune which to my young ears was a rather dour-sounding dirge (I later found out that it was written by none other than Irvin Berlin, but what would that have meant to a fourth-grader?).

> Give me your tired, your poor,
> Your huddled masses yearning to breathe free,
> The wretched refuse of your teeming shore.
> Send these, the homeless, tempest-tost to me,
> I lift my lamp beside the golden door.

The mention of "wretched refuse," which sounds terribly politically incorrect by today's standards, prompted Jerry Seinfeld to remark:

> Do we have to specify "The wretched refuse?" Why not just say, "Give us the unhappy, the sad, the slow, the ugly, the people that can't drive, people that have trouble merging ..."[1]

1. "Seinfeld Monologues," laughbreak.com/quotes/seinfeld-monologues/

What Emma Lazarus meant, of course, was the "unfortunate." Coming from a Portuguese Jewish family, she reflected in her poetry the Jewish value of *hakhnasat orchim*, hospitality or welcoming strangers—whether they are wretched, bad parkers, or anything else.

To be sure, welcoming guests is not a value unique to Jews. My Jewish uncle married into an Italian Catholic family and when we were invited over to eat, who could tell the difference between the Italians and the Jews? First came the salads, then came the sausages (not so Jewish, that), then came the chicken, then the pasta, the cole slaw, the bread. And just when it seemed impossible to get in one more bite, came the inevitable line: "Did you leave room for dessert?" We weren't sure if we were being offered hakhnasat orchim at that point or were part of a plot to kill us with food and then take over the world.

It seems that hospitality over meals is a human value. But hakhnasat orchim extends to much more than food. One Jewish writer brought the sentiment of Emma Lazarus' verse into the twenty-first century when he said, "Because of my religious beliefs, it is my mission to advocate for the Syrian refugees."[2] In other words, hospitality isn't just for when Uncle Sid and Aunt Gussie show up for dinner, invited or not; it's for the downtrodden of all times and places. Or take the fact that in August of 2015, the Israeli consulate in Shanghai released a video entitled, "Thank You Shanghai" in which Israel's Prime Minister Benjamin Netanyahu is heard saying, "When cities across the globe closed their doors to Jews fleeing genocide, Shanghai showed hospitality."[3]

In between a single meal and far-flung humanitarian crises, welcoming guests can comprise anything from offering couch surfers accommodations to having a neighbor's child over for a meal. But how exactly to show hospitality?

---

2. Avi Sholkoff, "Hachnasat Orchim: What a Jewish Value Can Teach Us About the Syrian Refugee Crisis," www.huffingtonpost.com/avi-sholkoff/hachnasat-orchim_b_8587164.html
3. Shiryn Solny, "New Video Shows Israelis Thanking Shanghai for Sheltering Jewish WWII Refugees," www.algemeiner.com/2015/08/28/new-video-shows-israelis-thanking-shanghai-for-sheltering-jewish-wwii-refugees/

The Secret Jewish Life of Miss Manners

Imagine a Jewish version of Miss Manners—we'll call her Mrs. Mentsch—receiving a query such as, "I'm Jewish. My husband says we should just invite guests in and tell them to make themselves at home. I think that as hosts, we should be doing more. What do you say?"

Mrs. Mentsch, in her own distinctive style, replies as follows (the italicized phrases are traditional Jewish requirements—requirements, not suggestions—for being a good host[4]):

> Are you kidding me? You listen to me because, to the contrary, Jewish tradition gives us plenty of guidance on being a welcoming host. Tell your husband that first of all, a good host *goes to the door* to welcome guests. Even if it's unlocked. What, he can't be bothered to get up? And another thing. He has to try and *stay upbeat and cheerful the whole time* his guests are there. Yes, this means he has to smile and show interest even if Gloria and Dominick (you didn't say, but I'm assuming an intermarried couple, why not?) are boring him with the minutiae of how they had a conniption trying to decide on granite or Formica for their kitchen counter. Of course, he should *offer something to eat and drink* but being Jewish, that just comes with the territory. But then you have a great trade-off. If G & D are busy devouring hors d'oevres, they can't talk as much. But that doesn't let him off the hook, because he needs to *ask them questions* about things they are interested in. "Tell me all about the first time little Hershey ate Cheerios." And at the end of the evening, he should *walk them to the door* on their way out—which, judging from the kind of person he seems to be, he will probably be all too eager to do. Just tell him not to walk too quickly. Because he's also *not supposed to make them uncomfortable*.

All the guidelines in italics go back at least to the Talmud, which means at least to around 550 C.E. if not earlier. But there's a flip

4. See Wendy Mogel, "Honoring Guests," www.kveller.com/article/honoring-guests/

side. Besides being a good host, one also must be a good guest. For example, overstaying one's welcome is not good. One frequently quoted saying has it that "on the day a guest arrives, a calf is slaughtered in his honor; the next day, a sheep; the third day, a fowl; and on the fourth day, he is served just beans!"[5] Hopefully, the by-then unwelcome visitor has gotten the point. What happens if he is still there on the fifth day is left unsaid. Even more pointedly, we are told that "houseguests and fish spoil on the third day."[6] The lesson seems to be that both may be thrown out.

And a good guest shows gratitude. When I was a child, the doctor's waiting room was filled with copies of a magazine called *Highlights for Children*, each issue of which had an illustrated column about two kids, "Gallant and Goofus." Gallant exemplified impeccably good behavior. Goofus, on the other hand, was a real pain in the *tuchus*—I'm guessing because his parents named him Goofus in the first place. Whether or not his mischievous behavior was due to his unfortunate name, it was clear that we were not to emulate him.

In Jewish tradition, it turns out that in being a guest, we can follow either our inner Gallant or Goofus. Gallant says, "How much trouble my host has taken for me! How much meat, wine, and cakes he has set before me!" But Goofus says, "How much effort did my host make for me? I have eaten [only] one piece of bread, I have eatedn [only] one slice of meat, and I have drunk [only] one cup of wine! Whatever trouble my host has taken was only for the sake of his wife and his children!"[7] In a way, Gallant is a glass half-full person, Goofus, a glass half-empty. But it goes beyond that. Goofus is simply ungrateful. And suspicious of motives. And probably resentful of his name.

This long-standing emphasis on hospitality finds it roots, as most Jewish values do, in the Hebrew Bible, starting with one of its most well-known characters, Abraham.

---

5. *Tehillim R.* 23:3, cited in Ronald L. Eisenberg, *The JPS Guide to Jwish Traditions* (Philadelphia: Jewish Publication Society, 2004), p. 542.

6. Nathan Ausubel, *A Treasury of Jewish Folklore: Stories, Traditions, Legends, Humor, Wisdom and Folk Songs of the Jewish People* (New York: Crown, 1948), p. 639.

7. Gallant and Goofus wouldn't have phrased it that way, but the Talmud does in *b. Berakhot* 58a, cited in Eisenberg, *JPS* Guide, p. 541.

Abraham, the Host Who Left God Waiting

In reading about Jewish hospitality, one cannot fail to come across the story of Abraham and his three guests, which is found in Genesis 18:1-8. Let's hear the whole story:

> The Lord appeared to him by the terebinths of Mamre; he was sitting at the entrance of the tent as the day grew hot. Looking up, he saw three men standing near him. As soon as he saw them, he ran from the entrance of the tent to greet them and, bowing to the ground, he said,
>
> "My lords, if it please you, do not go on past your servant. Let a little water be brought; bathe your feet and recline under the tree. And let me fetch a morsel of bread that you may refresh yourselves; then go on—seeing that you have come your servant's way."
>
> They replied, "Do as you have said."
>
> Abraham hastened into the tent to Sarah, and said, "Quick, three seahs of choice flour! Knead and make cakes!"
>
> Then Abraham ran to the herd, took a calf, tender and choice, and gave it to a servant-boy, who hastened to prepare it. He took curds and milk and the calf that had been prepared and set these before them; and he waited on them under the tree as they ate.

With typical Middle Eastern touches, Abraham bows, insists that the guests stay, tends to washing their feet (traveling with sandals and dust makes for tired, worn-out feet) and in quick order gets a meal ready. Like the servants on *Downton Abbey*, he also stands by ready to meet whatever needs arise. The insistence on inviting people to stay and eat a meal remains with Jews to this day.

Jewish tradition spins the biblical account in such a way as to emphasize the importance of hospitality—just to be sure we get the point. Abraham, we are to understand, was in the middle of talking with God ("the Lord appeared to him") when the guests arrived ("Looking up, he saw three men"). So important was it to be hospitable that Abraham, according to this interpretation, left

God standing there and went to take care of his visitors:[8] "Just a moment, God, I've got guests."

In reading the rest of the story, God wasn't really left to his own devices—the fact that Abraham saw three men explains *how* God appeared to Abraham (one or more of the visitors seems to have been God himself or an angel/angels). But the alternative reading makes a point: how important hakhnasat orchim really is. We can tell God to have a seat and wait while we attend to our guests—at least according to this tradition.

From Egypt to Elisha

While Abraham's behavior has become the paradigm of hospitality in Jewish thought, it is from a later time—when the Jewish nation had come into being—that the value of hakhnasat orchim is raised to a new level.

Some centuries after Abraham, the Jewish people found themselves as slaves in the land of Egypt. It is this very situation that gives the Bible its rationale for the value of hospitality.

Leviticus 19:34 enjoins, "The stranger who resides with you shall be to you as one of your citizens; you shall love him as yourself, for you were strangers in the land of Egypt."

Jews, in other words, know what it is like to be an outsider, to be mistreated, to be longing for a human touch, to want relationships based on love not fear. "You've been there and I, God, took you away from all that. Now treat others like I treated you." No wonder every Passover seder, with this back story in mind, includes the line, "Let all who are hungry, come and eat."[9]

In Jewish tradition, letting all the hungry come and eat was applied first to Passover itself. The custom of *maot hittim* (or *hittin*; the phrase means "wheat money") provides for giving money to poor Jews so that they can purchase or bake *matzah* for Passover;

8. See e.g., "Hospitality: Look Who's Coming for Dinner!", www.chabad.org/library/article_cdo/aid/691769/jewish/Hospitality.htm

9. Cf. *b. Taanit* 20b: "When [Rab Huna] had a meal he would open the door wide and declare, Whosoever is in need let him come and eat." Soncino edition.

in some times and places, food itself was distributed.[10] Today one can donate to a *maot hittim* fund for this same purpose.

But hospitality extends far beyond Passover. An article in the *Huffington Post* suggested that another application is support for child nutrition across the nation.[11] Since we know, at least in imagination, what is was like to be "strangers" in Egypt, we should extend ourselves to others in unfortunate situations.

And so we find that hospitality infuses many other biblical stories. Abraham's nephew Lot prevails on two angelic visitors to stay with him overnight.[12] Job, the sufferer *par excellence* of the Bible (he suffers from boils for almost forty-two chapters) insists that he has always opened his home to travelers.[13] Abraham's servant, setting off to find a wife for Abraham's son Isaac, encounters Rebekah and her brother Laban, who offers a place for both the servant and his camels.[14] Moses' future father-in-law Reuel, also known as Jethro, berates his daughters for not inviting Moses in for a meal.[15] An affluent woman living in the town of Shunem sets up a hospitality suite for the prophet Elisha's frequent travels through the area (2 Kings 4:8-11).[16] While all this could be written off simply as Middle Eastern tradition—"that's just how we roll here in the desert"—we have seen that there was a deeper reason for the imperative to be hospitable.

One Day at Good Samaritan Hospital

As we might imagine by now, the imperative of hospitality carries over into the New Testament. Here is a story that is found in Luke 10:25-37. It involves a conversation between Jesus and an "expert in Torah" but then quickly turns into a travelogue:

---

10. See Ronald H. Isaacs, "Maot Hittin: Wheat Money," www.myjewishlearning.com/article/maot-hittin-wheat-money/
11. Steve Gutow, "A Seder Lesson: Let All Who Are Hungry Come And Eat," www.huffingtonpost.com/rabbi-steve-gutow/let-all-who-are-hungry-co_b_520203.html
12. Genesis 19:1-3.
13. Job 31:32.
14. Genesis 24:28-32.
15. Exodus 2:20.
16. All these examples come from Eisenberg, *JPS Guide*, pp. 539-41.

> An expert in *Torah* stood up to try and trap him by asking, "Rabbi, what should I do to obtain eternal life?" But Yeshua said to him, "What is written in the *Torah*? How do you read it?" He answered, **"You are to love *ADONAI* your God with all your heart, with all your soul, with all your strength** and with all your understanding; and **your neighbor as yourself**."
>
> "That's the right answer," Yeshua said. "Do this, and you will have life."
>
> But he, wanting to justify himself, said to Yeshua, "And who is my '**neighbor**'?"
>
> Taking up the question, Yeshua said: "A man was going down from Yerushalyim to Yericho [Jerusalem to Jericho] when he was attacked by robbers. They stripped him naked and beat him up, then went off, leaving him half dead. By coincidence, a *cohen* was going down on that road; but when he saw him, he passed by on the other side. Likewise a *Levi* who reached the place and saw him also passed by on the other side.
>
> "But a man from Shomron [Samaria] who was traveling came upon him; and when he saw him, he was moved with compassion. So he went up to him, put oil and wine on his wounds and bandaged them. Then he set him on his own donkey, brought him to an inn and took care of him. The next day, he took out two days' wages, gave them to the innkeeper and said, 'Look after him; and if you spend more than this, I'll pay you back when I return.' Of these three, which one seems to you to have become the '**neighbor**' of the man who fell among robbers?"
>
> He answered, "The one who showed mercy toward him."
>
> Yeshua said to him, "You go and do as he did."[17]

As in many of Jesus' stories, you can't tell the players without a program. Here is the lineup of the characters in Luke's story, in order of appearance.

17. Luke 10:25-37. Boldface original.

First, we have an "expert in Torah," sometimes translated as a "lawyer." Luke uses this word, not to refer to those who argued cases in court, but to mean "scribes," who occupied a multifaceted profession in first-century Israel. (The Jewish surname Sofer or Sofaer means "scribe.") Scribes were multi-taskers: they wrote down scrolls of the Scripture, acted as teachers of the Torah and tradition and as here in Luke, were known for legal decision-making. Their work was pro bono and many took on a trade to support themselves. We know of scribes who sold wine, did carpentry and engaged in leather-work. But chiefly, they knew the law—the interpretations, the precedents, the subtleties that inform the legal profession to this day.

Next, we have a traveler and robbers. The Jerusalem-to-Jericho route was the kind of road your mother would have told you to avoid. Its 17-mile length was pockmarked with caves providing convenient cover for thieves waiting in ambush. Despite its danger, presumably the road was travelled enough to make it worth the while of thieves to hang out and await their prey.

The final characters are a priest, a Levite and a Samaritan. A priest (in Hebrew, *kohen*, hence the surname Cohen, Kahn and other derivations) officiated at the rituals involving sacrifices in the Jerusalem Temple and performed an assortment of other functions.

Levites (hence the surname Levi, Levy, Levine and other variations) acted as assistants to the priests and often provided the music at festivals and other occasions.

Samaritans were a group who were partly Jewish and had a rival holy site, Mount Gerizim instead of Jerusalem. Jews and Samaritans, like oil and water, did not mix either socially or theologically. Though both groups were on the same page in accepting the authority of the Torah, the Samaritans didn't accept the authority of the rest of the Hebrew Bible. Conflicts were not uncommon, sometimes ending up in fisticuffs requiring Rome to step in and separate the two.

Jesus' story is meant to surprise, perhaps to shock and to radicalize the idea of hospitality. The priest, perhaps, did not wish to engage with what he may have taken to be a corpse and thereby to render himself ritually impure according to biblical law. Or perhaps he saw that the man was still alive but couldn't be bothered. The Levite likewise may have had similar reasons. One might have expected the third character in the story to be an "Israelite," that is, a non-priest and non-Levite who would not risk ritual defilement in this situation and would step in to save the day. But Jesus throws a curve ball and the character turns out to be a Samaritan, whose act of compassion and hospitality is unexpected in this situation. Well, says Jesus, if a *Samaritan* could act like this towards a Jew, who is *your* neighbor?

From this story, by the way, comes the phrase "Good Samaritan," referring to someone who steps into a situation in an over-and-above way and renders help.

Jesus Goes to a Seder

The value of extending hospitality abounds in the New Testament in story and precept. Jesus and his twelve disciples were constantly on the move and relied on the hospitality of others, typical for a traveling rabbi and his band of followers. "When you come to a town or village, look for someone trustworthy and stay with him until you leave,"[18] Jesus instructs the dozen. What seems like an imposition to us was part and parcel of the social fabric in the first century.

And as we have seen, what better time to open up one's home than for Passover ? One unnamed person did so for Jesus and his followers:

> On the first day for *matzah*, when they slaughtered the lamb for *Pesach* [Passover], Yeshua's *talmidim* asked him, "Where do you want us to go and prepare your *Seder*?"
>
> He sent two of his disciples with these instructions: "Go into the city, and a man carrying a jar of water will meet you. Follow him; and whichever house he enters, tell him that the Rabbi says, 'Where is the guest room for me, where I am to eat the *Pesach* meal with my *talmidim*?' He

18. Matthew 10:11.

> will show you a large room upstairs, furnished and ready. Make the preparations there."
>
> The *talmidim* went off, came to the city and found things just as he had told them they would be; and they prepared the *Seder*.[19]

Evidently this was all pre-arranged. While the name of the homeowner has been lost to history, two-story homes with large "upper rooms" would mark the owner as affluent. This would be in the "better" part of town, the Upper City, while the Lower City was so to speak on the other side of the tracks and, as one commentator put it, "downwind of Jerusalem's sewage."[20] So Jesus and his entourage were able to have Passover in a nice house, with perhaps the homeowner present.

Beyond Fiction and Festivals

Hakhnasat orchim in the New Testament was not meant to be extended on a one-off occasion but to be part of the warp and woof of life.

"Share what you have with God's people, and practice hospitality," says Paul to a congregation made up of Jews and Gentiles in Rome.[21] "Welcome one another into your homes without grumbling," insists Peter.[22] We have already seen that being good hosts and guests means having a good attitude. It's not real hospitality to invite someone in and be muttering under your breath about them.

The book of Hebrews puts hospitality on the same level as showing brotherly love and remembering prisoners:

> Let brotherly friendship continue; but don't forget to be friendly to outsiders; for in so doing, some people, without knowing it, have entertained angels. Remember those in

19. Mark 14:12-16.
20. Keener, *IVP Bible Background Commentary*, to Mark 14:14-16.
21. Romans 12:13.
22. 1 Peter 4:9.

> prison and being mistreated, as if you were in prison with them and undergoing their torture yourselves.[23]

Hebrews seems to be referring us back to the story of Abraham and his three visitors, who turned out to be more than just ordinary travelers. And with this, we have come full circle. Hakhnasat orchim is a thread that runs from the Hebrew Bible through Jewish tradition and on into the New Testament. Abraham would have approved—and would probably have offered Jesus and his apostles a meal.

23. Hebrews 13:1-3.

Chapter 6

Care of Widows and Orphans

(Almanot v'Yetomim)

If you take a poll as to who the most famous orphan of all time is, you may find that Little Orphan Annie, the heroine of the twentieth-century American comic strip of the same name, heads the list. Despite her semi-iconic status and the fact that an upbeat Broadway musical was based on her adventures, she had the disturbing feature that her big white eyes had no pupils. Neither did the peepers of her dog, Sandy, or her sponsor "Daddy" Warbucks. Maybe that's why Mrs. Warbucks always wanted to send her back to the orphanage. Except that Mrs. Warbucks probably suffered from the same malady. The whole lot of them probably should have paid a visit to the ophthalmologist.

I don't know that the next candidate would make it in a general poll, but there is another famous orphan in the book of Esther, the events of which underlie the holiday of Purim. You may know the cast of characters in this story: there is the almost unpronounceable Ahasuerus, king of Persia; Mordecai, a Jewish man living in the city of Susa; Haman, who ends up plotting to destroy all the Jews; and Mordecai's cousin Hadassah, or Esther.

> He was foster father to Hadassah—that is, Esther—his uncle's daughter, for she had neither father nor mother. The

> maiden was shapely and beautiful; and when her father and mother died, Mordecai adopted her as his own daughter.[1]

Under encouragement from Mordecai, Hadassah aka Esther dared to enter the king's presence, reveal Haman's genocidal plot and save the Jewish people from certain annihilation. The holiday of Purim ensued, during which we cheer Mordecai and boo Haman, though truth be told, it may be Esther who really deserves the cheering.

As far as the most well-known among widows goes, in recent decades we can perhaps dubiously include the Little Old Lady from Pasadena, whose escapades as recorded by the Beach Boys and others can still be heard online.

It seems that in 1964, Dodge automobile ran TV ads in which a grey-haired older lady sped around town in her Dodge. We are given to believe that Pasadena widows would inherit their cars from their deceased husbands, yet rarely drove them, hence the old joke that the used car you had your eye on "was only driven by a little old lady on Sundays." The Little Old Lady of the song, however, couldn't "keep her foot off the accelerator" and raced like a maniac around town to the chorus of "Go granny, go granny, go granny go!" Go to jail, is probably more like it; as far as I can tell, she seemed to be the kind of person who ran red lights and led the police on highway chases.

While Esther rose to be queen of Persia, Annie starred in her very own comic strip, and the Little Old Lady had a song written about her, most who have lost spouses or parents end up neither as royalty nor as pop culture icons. The life of Charles Dickens' character Oliver Twist, another iconic orphan, was delineated with harsh realism, making real for countless readers the exploitation of children, and especially orphans, in nineteenth-century England.

In real life, as opposed to surf music, becoming spouseless and parentless entails grief, life reorganization, social relocation

1. Esther 2:7.

and in some times and places, increased vulnerability. Knowing what this kind of loss can mean, a 2012 survey[2] revealed that 80% of American Jews reported that "caring for the widow and the orphan" was "somewhat or very important" to them.

A third kind of person, the "stranger" or "sojourner," is sometimes thrown in for good measure along with the widow and the orphan. This, I hasten to add, is not the kind of stranger you taught your children to avoid. Rather, it refers to someone living short- or long-term in Israel, who wasn't fully part of Jewish society but nevertheless needed tangible help.

The Seder Connection

We've seen how the Passover experience underlies several Jewish values. Care for widows and orphans forms yet another example:

> For the LORD your God is God supreme and Lord supreme, the great, the mighty, and the awesome God, who shows no favor and takes no bribe, but upholds the cause of the fatherless and the widow, and befriends the stranger, providing him with food and clothing.—You too must befriend the stranger, for you were strangers in the land of Egypt.[3]

The remembrance that we were strangers in Egypt forms part of every year's Passover seder. (If your family was the kind that wondered how much of the Haggadah you could skip before you could eat, you may have missed that part.) Though we were slaves, we are also described as temporary residents, living in our very own Jewish neighborhood called Goshen. Goshen was not a ghetto; it was more like a suburban area, the place where Joseph brought his family to live in when they were still

2. Robert P. Jones, Daniel Cox, *Chosen for What? Jewish Values in 2012: Findings from the 2012 Jewish Values Survey* (Washington, DC: Public Religion Research Institute, Inc., 2012), www.prri.org/research/jewish-values-in-2012/

3. Deut. 10:17-19.

able to freely move around in Egypt. And that is where the Jews remained, even after a new Pharaoh came to power who enslaved them all.

The idea is that just as God heard our cry in slavery, so he will hear the cry of afflicted widows. But can slavery possibly compare with being a temporary resident, an orphan or a widow? Yet there it is. The same Hebrew words translated *afflict*[4] and *cry*[5] are used for both situations:

> Slaves: "You took note of our fathers' affliction in Egypt, and heard their cry at the Sea of Reeds."[6]
>
> The husbandless and the orphan: "You shall not ill-treat any widow or orphan. If you do mistreat them, I will heed their outcry as soon as they cry out to Me."[7]

The correlation makes more sense when we consider that in past times and still in some places outside the West, widows and orphans could end up in financial slavery, unable to pay their debts or meet their basic needs. Moreover, emotional affliction could be and still can be, a real part of widowhood and fatherlessness. Slavery, affliction, being without father or husband—in many ways the boundary can be blurred.

And so back to the seder. When a widow or an orphan receives justice and protection, they are in a real way experiencing their own personal Passover, their moment of redemption. I have never seen a special haggadah for widows and orphans, but it might be very appropriate.[8] It might even slow down your family from asking, "When do we get to eat?"

---

4. *'anah* and related forms of the word.
5. *tza'aq* or its alternate *za'aq*.
6. Nehemiah 9:9. See also Deuteronomy 26:7.
7. Ex. 22:21-22 (verses 22-23 in other English translations).
8. Some Jewish homes for orphans did issue haggadot for their supporters and included pictures of their facilities and the children.

Baldy Fills Up Some Jars

The quote above from Deuteronomy isn't just a one-off. It is the constant reiteration in Bible that underlies its inclusion as a chief Jewish value:

> Cursed be he who subverts the rights of the stranger, the fatherless, and the widow.[9]
> Learn to do good.
> Devote yourselves to justice;
> Aid the wronged.
> Uphold the rights of the orphan;
> Defend the cause of the widow.[10]
> Judge the wretched and the orphan,
> vindicate the lowly and the poor.[11]

These were not just pious platitudes. Some stories picture the plight of the powerless very concretely.

We briefly met the prophet Elisha in a previous chapter. Elisha, it turns out, was something of a miracle worker. For what it's worth, he was also apparently bald, as we learn from his encounter with some neighborhood toughs (a better translation than the following "little boys" as rendered in the JPS version): "As he was going up the road, some little boys came out of the town and jeered at him, saying, 'Go away, baldhead! Go away, baldhead!'"[12] Shaved heads were apparently not cool back then and miraculously summoning a toupee did not seem to be in Elisha's repertoire.

What *was* in his repertoire, though, was care for a widow. We encounter Elisha once again in 2 Kings 4:

> A certain woman, the wife of one of the disciples of the prophets, cried out to Elisha: "Your servant my husband is dead, and you know how your servant revered the LORD.

9. Deuteronomy 27:19; see also Deuteronomy 24:17.
10. Isaiah 1:17; see also Jeremiah 22:3.
11. Psalm 82:3.
12. 2 Kings 2:23.

> And now a creditor is coming to seize my two children as slaves."
>
> Elisha said to her, "What can I do for you? Tell me, what have you in the house?"
>
> She replied, "Your maidservant has nothing at all in the house, except a jug of oil."
>
> "Go," he said, "and borrow vessels outside, from all your neighbors, empty vessels, as many as you can. Then go in and shut the door behind you and your children, and pour [oil] into all those vessels, removing each one as it is filled."
>
> She went away and shut the door behind her and her children. They kept bringing [vessels] to her and she kept pouring. When the vessels were full, she said to her son, "Bring me another vessel." He answered her, "There are no more vessels"; and the oil stopped.
>
> She came and told the man of God, and he said, "Go sell the oil and pay your debt, and you and your children can live on the rest."[13]

Miracles like these were not meant primarily to dazzle and impress, but to show God's care for the unfortunate in providing for their needs.[14]

From the Talmud to Treblinka

After the days of the Hebrew Bible, Jewish tradition continued to stress the importance of caring for widows and orphans using a variety of images and insights. With a legal metaphor, the Talmud refers to judges as "fathers of orphans,"[15] the point being that in lieu of actual fathers, the legal system ideally would step in to offer the missing protection.

13. 2 Kings 4:1-7.

14. It's interesting that a similar "miracle of oil" is associated with the holiday of Hanukkah. There, it has to do with getting the worship of the entire nation back on its feet in the Temple; here, the concern is with a single individual.

15. *b. Baba Kamma* 37a.

Famed medieval sage and medical doctor Maimonides offered psychological insight when he wrote

> A man ought to be especially heedful of his behavior toward widows and orphans, for their souls are exceedingly depressed and their spirits low. Even if they are wealthy, even if they are the widows and orphans of a king, we are specifically enjoined concerning them.[16]

Besides direct commands and psychological insight, a third approach to our topic involved word-play, and was offered by nineteenth-century rabbi Samson Raphael Hirsch in his explanation of the Hebrew word for "widow." This term, *almanah*, derives from *illem*, meaning "dumb, speechless." *Yatom*, the word for orphan, comes from a word implying mutilation. Hirsch interpreted this to mean that a widow no longer has anyone to speak up for her (especially true in former times when the status of women was not what it is today in the West), while an orphan's hand has been figuratively cut off since there is no father to lead with a helping hand. He concludes that the vulnerable of society need to be given both a voice and strength to live.[17]

Given all this concern for widows and orphans, it is not surprising that the late 19th and early 20th centuries saw the heyday of special Jewish societies for orphans as well as those who lost husbands. In response to the great need, widows' and orphans' institutions multiplied like Jewish rabbits, all bearing names disclosing their niche. There are dozens if not hundreds; my favorite name is that of a Brooklyn-based outfit, the Friendly Home for Girls. These institutions provided not only for orphans, but for any children whose parents were unable to care for them—underscoring that this Jewish value is really about *all* the vulnerable.[18]

16. Telushkin, *Jewish Literacy*, p. 503.
17. "Widows & Orphans—Mishpatim," bitly.com/widows-orphans
18. See an extensive listing of such organizations at David Ballela, "The Site of the Israel Orphan Asylum," knickerbockervillage.blogspot.com/2008/12/site-of-israel-orphan-asylum.html

But perhaps the most poignant account of care for orphans concerns an orphanage located in the Warsaw Ghetto, run by author and medical doctor Janusz Korczak. In an exemplary instance of showing care for his charges, he refused offers of sanctuary for himself. Along with other leaders in the orphanage, he accompanied the children when they were deported to the concentration camp of Treblinka in 1942, holding the children's hands as together they marched to their deaths. One can hardly think of a more sacrificial way of showing care for orphans.[19]

The Fighting Widow

Mistreatment of widows seems unfortunately to have been more common than one would like. Another such widow, let's call her Mrs. Needleman, appears in one of Jesus' parables (stories based around common life experiences that ended with a spiritual point). This is a story that would have resonated with many Jews who first heard it:

> Then Yeshua told his *talmidim* a parable, in order to impress on them that they must always keep praying and not lose heart. "In a certain town, there was a judge who neither feared God nor respected other people. There was also in that town a widow who kept coming to him and saying, 'Give me a judgment against the man who is trying to ruin me.' For a long time he refused; but after awhile, he said to himself, 'I don't fear God, and I don't respect other people; but because this widow is such a *nudnik* [pest], I will see to it that she gets justice—otherwise, she'll keep coming and pestering me till she wears me out!'"
>
> Then the Lord commented, "Notice what this corrupt judge says. Now, won't God grant justice to his chosen people who cry out to him day and night? Is he delaying long over them? I tell you that he will judge in their favor,

19. See e.g., "Janusz Korczak (1878–1942)," www.jewishvirtuallibrary.org/janusz-korczak

> and quickly! But when the Son of Man comes, will he find this trust on the earth at all?"[20]

The parable is illustrative not only of the common plight of widows but apparently also of the failure of the justice system to be of any help. In this case, however, Mrs. Needleman gets the better of the judge basically by being a royal nag.

"Wear me out" in verse 5 may be too understated of a translation. The Greek expression means something like "give me a black eye." Mrs. Needleman is no pushover. The judge's response, to give it a more modern spin, was along the lines of, "this *ferkakte* [a Yiddish adjective suggesting great displeasure] widow keeps bugging the heck out of me, so I better issue a ruling before she gives me a black eye!"

The point about justice is incidental to the main point, which is about praying to God. Using a typical Jewish way of reasoning—from a lesser thing to a greater thing—the upshot is that if an *unjust* judge finally dispenses justice because the plaintiff is being a pain, how much more will the *just* God provide justice if we keep asking him? People may not live up to the ideal, but God will. After all, most Jewish values can be traced back to the Bible and so to God—and we can expect that he will follow the ideals that he himself has established.

Widowed and Almost Childless

The previous two examples—the widow and Elisha, and the nagging widow—told about injustice to widows. There is a third story which gives us a contrasting positive example: Jesus' care for a widow, both materially and emotionally, showing how he embodied this core value. The story concerns a dramatic miracle:

> The next day Yeshua, accompanied by his *talmidim* and a large crowd, went to a town called Na'im. As he

20. Luke 18:1-8.

> approached the town gate, a dead man was being carried out for burial. His mother was a widow, this had been her only son, and a sizeable crowd from the town was with her. When the Lord saw her, he felt compassion for her and said to her, "Don't cry."
>
> Then he came close and touched the coffin, and the pallbearers halted. He said, "Young man, I say to you: get up!" The dead man sat up and began to speak, and Yeshua **gave him to his mother**. They were all filled with awe and gave glory to God, saying, "A great prophet has appeared among us," and, "God has come to help his people."[21]

Na'im, or Nain, was a town in northern Israel, in the Galilee region, which still exists today southwest of the Sea of Galilee. Its name come from the Hebrew for "pleasant," but the situation described here was anything but.

A widow—this time we'll call her The Widow Waldbaum—having already lost her husband, had now lost her only son. This was a personal loss as well as an economic one; her son would have been a source of financial support. Since we read that a large crowd was accompanying her on the way (we assume) to the burial, the Nainites evidently provided an emotional support group for her.

What is interesting is that as Jesus was coming in the opposite direction, there was also a large crowd with him. This means that there was quite a sizable group as both parties converged. Evidently The Widow Waldbaum was well-known and had an extended network of friends and acquaintances who cared enough to visit her. Once the two groups meet up, Jesus then works a miracle and raises Waldbaum Jr. from the dead, thereby both restoring the relationship and providing for her ongoing needs—and demonstrating God's power to the combined groups.

21. Luke 7:11-16. Boldface original.

Not many people will end up raising someone from the dead, but the Jewish value of care for widows can take other forms, as we will now see.

The Day the Widows Didn't Eat Lunch

After Jesus died and, according to the New Testament, rose from the dead, the Jesus-movement began to grow. At one point, the treatment of widows again proved noteworthy:

> Around this time, when the number of *talmidim* was growing, the Greek-speaking Jews began complaining against those who spoke Hebrew that their widows were being overlooked in the daily distribution. So the Twelve called a general meeting of the *talmidim* and said,
>
> "It isn't appropriate that we should neglect the Word of God in order to serve tables. Brothers, choose seven men from among yourselves who are known to be full of the Spirit and wisdom. We will appoint them to be in charge of this important matter, but we ourselves will give our full attention to praying and to serving the Word."[22]

First, in the *Playbill* of this story, we have the cast of characters to figure out: "Greek-speaking" Jews are those from the Diaspora, originally from outside Israel but now living in the Land, the equivalent of American or French Jews who've made aliyah. "Those who spoke Hebrew" are the *sabras*, those born and raised in Israel. The "Twelve" are the original twelve apostles of Jesus whom we meet in the gospel accounts, although by this time Judas—the traitorous Benedict Arnold of the Jesus story—has been replaced by someone else.

Next after the cast is the plot, which I've updated slightly: The American Jewish widows who've made aliyah are being treated differently than the ones who've lived in Tel Aviv their whole lives.

---

22. Acts 6:1-4.

It seems that there were in fact a substantial number of Diaspora widows in Israel at that time, which is actually not too surprising. For one thing, many Jews made aliyah in order be buried in the Land and if they died in advance of their wives—a not infrequent occurrence, as is also the case today—often the women would be left as widows.

Others, following an old tradition, may have moved to Israel to get ready for the great resurrection when God would raise all the dead back to life at the end of time. This tradition stipulated that if someone died outside the Land, say in Minnesota or Tokyo or Barrow, Alaska (I will leave it to your imagination what Jews would be doing dying in Barrow), you would first have to roll underground all the way back to Israel in order to be resurrected.[23] Details of this ancient subway system are not to be found in the Bible, but in any event, it would have been much easier just to move to the Land while you were still alive.[24] And again, husbands statistically died before their wives, so *voilà*, once again there would be a surfeit of widows.

First-century synagogues in Israel, which provided support services to their members, were often organized according to area of geographical origin. The originally-Minnesotans had the Minnesota Minyan, the Tokyo Jews (don't ask—perhaps they went there for the sushi) had Temple Tokyo and the Jews from Ninevut met at Congregation Anshei Iceberg. It seems that even this network could not keep up with the overabundance of diaspora widows and the early movement of Jesus' followers suffered from this same stratification of social services. The problem was not one of deliberate maliciousness but of strained resources; in the running of the daily soup kitchen, the Diaspora widows were being "overlooked." The solution, as far as the Jesus-movement was concerned, was found in appointing special officials to be sure

---

23. See the very brief account at Ilana Sichel, "The Ancient Belief in Jewish Bones Tunneling to Jerusalem on Judgment Day," thejewniverse.com/2016/the-ancient-belief-in-jewish-bones-tunneling-to-jerusalem-on-judgment-day/

24. Compare this custom: "All Jews in the Diaspora get symbolically buried in Israel by having Israeli soil sprinkled into the coffin." At "Tahara Supplies for the Chevra Kadisha," www.jewish-funerals.org/tahara-supplies-chevra-kadisha

that all material needs were met.[25] In this way the biblical ideal of caring for widows was met.

Dorcas Was a Dear

On a personal level, we read of a woman who apparently showed a great deal of care for widows that she knew:

> Now in Yafo [Jaffa] there was a *talmidah* [female disciple] named Tavita (which means "gazelle"); she was always doing *tzedakah* and other good deeds. It happened that just at that time, she took sick and died. After washing her, they laid her in a room upstairs. Lud is near Yafo, and the *talmidim* had heard that Kefa [Peter] was there, so they sent two men to him and urged him, "Please come to us without delay." Kefa got up and went with them.
>
> When he arrived, they led him into the upstairs room. All the widows stood by him, sobbing and showing all the dresses and coats Tavita had made them while she was still with them. But Kefa put them all outside, kneeled down and prayed. Then, turning to the body, he said, "Tavita! Get up!" She opened her eyes; and on seeing Kefa, she sat up. He offered her his hand and helped her to her feet; then, calling the believers and the widows, he presented her to them alive. This became known all over Yafo, and many people put their trust in the Lord.[26]

Yafo or Jaffa is just north of modern Tel Aviv. This woman was a follower of Jesus whose name Tavita, often spelled Tabitha, meant "gazelle." So did the Greek equivalent, Dorcas, which many translations use in place of "gazelle." Her actions were as graceful as her name. Verse 39 indicates that she used to provide "all the widows" with homemade clothing. Whether as a personal project or in some official capacity, Tavita/Dorcas put into action the biblical

25. See Keener, *IVP Bible Background Commentary*, on Acts 6:2-4.
26. Acts 9:35b-42. Verses 36-42 in other English translations.

injunction to care for widows. When she died, Kefa (or Peter), one of the original apostles of Jesus, raised her from the dead. This was not only an act of compassion for Dorcas (and we presume for whoever was her family), but also, we can assume, she could now continue her benevolent work among the widows of Jaffa.

What Happened to the Orphans?

The New Testament's stories focus mainly on widows, while for whatever reason, orphans manage to appear only twice. Once the word appears in the gospel of John, in which Jesus tells his disciples that following his death and resurrection: "I will not leave you orphans—I am coming to you." (John 14:18; the way he will come to them turns out to be by sending "the Holy Spirit" to be with them.)

More pertinent to the Jewish value we are discussing is the book of James, which includes in its proverbial and ethical advice the following:

> The religious observance that God the Father considers pure and faultless is this: to care for orphans and widows in their distress and to keep oneself from being contaminated by the world.[27]

For whatever reasons, though orphans are continually mentioned in conjunction with widows, stories of orphans are rare in either the Hebrew Bible or the New Testament. Clearly, though, both widows and orphans were on the Jewish radar, for Moses, for Isaiah, for Jesus—and for us today.

27. James 1:27.

CHAPTER 7

CHARITY

(Tzedakah)

The Blue Box

Among its various meanings, *tzedakah* means charity. Though doing tzedakah is a Jewish value, giving to charity is of course not just a Jewish thing. Growing up, I could not escape the omnipresent hints to give to worthy causes. Seemingly every store had a cardboard coin collector for the March of Dimes, originally established to fight polio. These were not boxes but holders with pictures of needy people on them and spaces cut out in which dimes or quarters or nickels could be placed. It was hard to buy a candy bar or a comic book in such places without also thinking that there were less fortunate people who needed help. To this day, the dimes are still marching, though the cardboard collectors have largely gone the way of the Automat and the way of most who even remember what the Automat was.[1]

The Jewish National Fund's iconic "Blue Box," however, is one exception to the demise of the physical coin collector. The JNF has provided this famous tzedakah box—also known as a *pushke*—for over one hundred years. The venerable tin collector continues to be a vehicle for Jewish families to teach the value of giving and to ensure that something is set aside regularly for that purpose.

1. For the curious, see Carolyn Hughes Crowley, "Meet Me at the Automat," www.smithsonianmag.com/arts-culture/meet-me-at-the-automat-47804151/

And before there was a tin box, there was a felt hat—Theodor Herzl's hat, to be specific. The headpiece belonging to the founder of Zionism was passed around at the Fifth Zionist Congress of 1901 to raise monies for purchasing land in what was then called Palestine.[2] And prior to either a hat or a box for the home, tzedakah boxes were placed in public places, including synagogues or at the entrances to Jewish cemeteries. The home version apparently did not arise until around the 18th century.[3]

However, you do it, giving to charity is considered a core value of Judaism. There is a connection between justice and charitable giving. When you give tzedakah, you are promoting the cause of justice. As one pamphlet puts it, "'*Tzedaka*' is usually translated as 'charity,' but it comes from the word '*tzedek*' meaning justice. Giving *tzedaka* is not an act of generosity or mercy. It is an act of fairness. It's not a 'nice' thing to do; it's the *right* thing to do."[4]

Some like to trace the first tzedakah box to the ninth century B.C.E. when the Jewish king Jehoash went all *60 Minutes* and discovered that money intended for the upkeep and repair of the Temple was being used for other purposes. Whether that was a deliberate siphoning of funds or financial mismanagement we cannot say, but we do know what happened as a result. A priest named Jehoiada took a box, drilled a hole in it and made it the receptacle for future donations, with strict controls on how and when it could be opened. The story is found in the Bible, in 2 Kings 12:7-12.[5] There you have it. *Pushke 101*.

The tzedakah box has even had something of a literary career. In the 1930s, a children's book entitled *Blue-Box the Bold* was set in Israel. The box had the unusual property of turning itself into other objects, such as an armored vehicle whose wheels were made from pennies. It seems that Blue-Box the Bold was eventually

2. "JNF's Iconic Blue Box Redesigned," usa.jnf.org/about-jnf/jnfs-iconic-blue-box-1.html
3. "A History of the Charity Box," www.chabad.org/library/article_cdo/aid/390485/jewish/A-History-of-the-Charity-Box.htm
4. Jack Abramowitz, "Tzedaka," available at https://slideblast.com/queue/tzedaka_59afca0f1723dde08755e23d.html. Italicized word "right" was bolded in original.
5. In JPS version. Verses 6-11 in other English translations.

joined by several other boxy friends and all together, they were able to jump-start Jewish life in Israel.[6] Such is the power of the *pushke* and the value of charitable giving.

The Life and Times of Tzipporah Tzedakah

Tzipporah Tzedakah lives in the 21st century and for her, giving to charity is relatively easy to do. It doesn't take much for her to write a check or click a box in her online banking program. Some days she is more hands-on, serving in a local soup kitchen on Mondays and tutoring students after school on Thursdays; giving of one's time and knowledge is a form of charity, too. If you know some Hebrew, you will recognize that her name translates into English as Charity Bird. I think that's a great name for anyone, but in this chapter, we'll just call her Tzipporah.

Now suppose Tzipporah lived in, say, the tenth century B.C.E. Her tzedakah would take a much different form, as we glimpse from the laws of charitable giving in the Bible. For example, here's a law directed to farmers in ancient Israel, who formed a large proportion of the population:

> When you reap the harvest of your land, you shall not reap all the way to the edges of your field, or gather the gleanings of your harvest. You shall not pick your vineyard bare, or gather the fallen fruit of your vineyard; you shall leave them for the poor and the stranger: I the Lord am your God.[7]

Imagine a conversation between Tzipporah and her farmer husband, Self-Centered Shmuley:

> Shmuley: I have to get myself a better harvester. This one leaves a border around the field. It's doesn't get all the grapes! That's what I get for buying cheap.

6. Jenna Weissman Joselit, "When Pushke Came to Shove," www.forward.com/culture/14464/when-pushke-came-to-shove-02738/

7. Leviticus 19:9-10.

TZIPPORAH: You don't need a better harvester! The Torah says not to reap to the edges, anyway. Remember, we're supposed to leave them for the poor people.

SHMULEY: I haven't seen a poor person here in years!

TZIPPORAH: That's because you always go back and pick the parts the harvester didn't get and you also pick up everything that falls out of your hands while you carry it to the storage shed. *Of course,* there are no poor people around *our* farm!

SHMULEY: Ha! I like it that way! More grapes for us!

TZIPPORAH: If you eat any more grapes, your face will turn green.

SHMULEY: No, the other farmers' faces will turn green—green from envy, when they see how many crops *we've* taken in while they let the poor take advantage of *them*!

TZIPPORAH: You, my dear, are an idiot.

SHMULEY: But I'm an idiot with a lot of grapes.

Self-Centered Shmuley may or may not have been an idiot, but the Bible suggests that he is a big ingrate. After all, reasons the Scripture, God took us from slavery in Egypt and brought us into a land "flowing with milk and honey," which is to say, a land of magnificent abundance. (Our history in Egypt serves as rationale for several Jewish values: hospitality, as we saw in a previous chapter and now tzedakah.) It was God who gave the land to us when we as a nation were unfortunate and oppressed; this is why the law ends with "I the LORD am your God." How then can we ignore our unfortunate fellow Jews who live among us? For that matter, how can we ignore the "alien," the non-Jewish resident, who lived in Israel?

Lenders, Charity and *Gonifs*

Here is another law:

> If, however, there is a needy person among you, one of your kinsmen in any of your settlements in the land that the Lord your God is giving you, do not harden your heart and shut your hand against your needy kinsman. Rather, you must open your hand and lend him sufficient for whatever he needs. Beware lest you harbor the base thought, "The seventh year, the year of remission, is approaching," so that you are mean to your needy kinsman and give him nothing. He will cry out to the Lord against you, and you will incur guilt.[8]

This passage, which I have not quoted in its entirety, begins by putting us on notice us that all debts have to be cancelled at the end of every seventh year, called sabbatical years. (Today professors go on sabbaticals; back then loans did so, in a manner of speaking.) That was good news for poor people; it was God's enactment of nationwide charity and benevolence. The problem was that many people might refuse to lend money as the seventh year approached, knowing they would never be repaid.

The Bible therefore warns against doing just that and insists that those poor who have financial needs are to be extended those loans, sabbatical year or no sabbatical year. This, of course, puts a wrench in the whole lending thing. Tzipporah would have to forgive any loans not paid back by the end of the seventh year, trusting—as the Bible insists—that God will financially provide for those who abide by this law. Those loans would become a kind of mandatory charity. As it turns out, many people did refuse to extend loans in such circumstances.

The Scripture doesn't address what could be the opposite problem, namely, the case of someone who receives a loan and then hems and haws until the seventh year rolled around, insisting

8. Deuteronomy 15:7-9.

that they were not yet able to repay it. Presumably there were safeguards against this sort of thing, but we are not told about them. The Bible's emphasis is not on poor people who might abuse the laws that favored them, but on the haves doing the right thing for the have-nots. Some modern charities have come under scrutiny for mismanagement or fraud; we don't stop giving to charity because of them.

Not to be outdone, a few centuries later the prophet Amos spoke to price gouging and other unsavory practices that especially wreaked havoc on the lives of the poor.

> Listen to this, you who devour the needy, annihilating the poor of the land, saying, "If only the new moon were over, so that we could sell grain; the sabbath, so that we could offer wheat for sale, using an ephah that is too small, and a shekel that is too big, tilting a dishonest scale, and selling grain refuse as grain! We will buy the poor for silver, the needy for a pair of sandals." The LORD swears by the Pride of Jacob: "I will never forget any of their doings."[9]

The "New Moon" was the first of every month, which at that time was treated in many ways like the weekly Sabbath, a day when business was suspended. The merchants described here were the mirror images of charitable givers: they are connivers and robbers, *gonifs* (thieves) to the core. None of this was unique to ancient Israel; the ancient Code of Hammurabi talks about those who "use a light scale to measure the grain or the silver that they lend and a heavy scale to measure the grain or the silver that they collect."[10] But Israel had the experience of the Egyptian slavery and the rescue from that behind them, which should have informed their behavior. The "grain refuse" is the leftover wheat husks, inedible but added into the pile, much as if someone were to sell coffee

9. Amos 8:4-7.

10. John H. Walton, Victor Harold Matthews and Mark W. Chavalas, *The IVP Bible Background Commentary: Old Testament* (Downers Grove, Ill.: InterVarsity Press, 2000), on Amos 8:5.

beans mixed with, unknown to the purchaser, coffee plant leaves. Tzipporah would plotz.

The book of Proverbs sums it all up:

> He who withholds what is due to the poor affronts
> his Maker;
> He who shows pity for the needy honors Him.[11]

From Maimonides to Home Depot

The twelfth-century rabbi Maimonides was a doctor, a scholar and a philosopher of tzedakah. According to him, not all tzedakah is created equal. Just when you thought it was safe to write a check to your favorite charity, Maimonides enumerates eight levels of charitable giving, undoubtedly meant to encourage the most helpful kinds of tzedakah. The eight levels, from lowest to highest, are as follows,[12] with imagined remarks from the giver:

1. Giving, but with a bad attitude. "The Daughters of the French Revolution are knocking at the door again. Might as well give them a buck and get them off my back!"
2. Giving cheerfully but giving less than appropriate. "Glad to help the disaster relief in Japan! Here's a dime, pal!"
3. Giving, but only when asked. "Wanna give to the Human Fund?" "Um, sure, the Human Fund, OK …"
4. Giving without being asked, but the giver and the recipient each know who the other is. "Hey, Heshie, let me write you a check for your Save the Arctic Baboon fund." "Thanks, Morty!"
5. The giver does not know who the recipient is, but the recipient knows who the giver is. "Hey, let me write a check and I'll leave the "Payable to" line blank."

11. Proverbs 14:31.
12. See Abramowitz, "Tzedaka."

6. The recipient does not know who the giver is, but the giver knows who the recipient is. "Hey, let me give some cash to Heshie's Save the Arctic Baboon fund."
7. Neither the giver nor the recipient knows who the other one is. "Hey, let me give some cash to Frummy Golwitz, he'll know who to give it to."
8. Enabling the recipient to become self-reliant, for example by helping him get a job. "Hey, let me give to this micro-loan fund for self-sustaining farming in Ecuador."

Probably everyone would agree that the first on the list, giving with a lousy attitude, is not really all that great—though better than not giving at all. And number 8 is increasingly recognized as being better than just throwing money at problems. In between, few probably stop to analyze whether and why one kind of giving is "better" than another.

The idea of tzedakah extends beyond the idea of individuals helping other individuals. Philanthropy is tzedakah on a large scale and has played a prominent role in the Jewish community. The UJA-Federation,[13] founded in 1917, is one of the largest of Jewish philanthropic organizations. Some Jewish philanthropic giving falls under Maimonides' fourth type, where the giver and recipient both know one another; the recipient may be a hospital and the giver becomes known when the new wing is named "The Hershiker Annex." Then there is much that is anonymous.

One example of corporate philanthropy is the practice of Bernie Marcus, the Jewish founder of Home Depot, who notes that "that's tzedakah—when you do it and you don't look for the acknowledgments." That seems to fall somewhere in the middle of Maimonides' list—which does not mean that it's only middling tzedakah. Maimonides' eight levels, after all, did not come with a divine imprimatur. Whenever disaster strikes in the U.S., Home Depot does tzedakah by allowing first responders to take whatever

---

13. UJA Federation New York web site, www.ujafedny.org

equipment they need. They also function as a triage center for dropping off pets displaced by tornadoes or other disasters. You can hear Marcus talk about tzedakah here: watch.jerusalemu.org/home-depots-jewish-secret-to-success.

Jesus on Tzedakah

This continual thread of concern for giving tzedakah is reflected in the New Testament as well. Jesus seems to come down on the side of Maimonides' sixth and seventh levels. Of course, that is an anachronism since Maimonides lived more than a thousand years after Jesus. Had Maimonides and Jesus been able to sit down, perhaps over a nice cup of espresso in Egypt (where Maimonides was a physician), they probably would have had a lot to talk about. Here is Jesus on doing tzedakah:

> "Be careful not to parade your acts of *tzedakah* in front of people in order to be seen by them! If you do, you have no reward from your Father in heaven. So, when you do *tzedakah*, don't announce it with trumpets to win people's praise, like the hypocrites in the synagogues and on the streets. Yes! I tell you, they have their reward already! But you, when you do *tzedakah*, don't even let your left hand know what your right hand is doing. Then your *tzedakah* will be in secret; and your Father, who sees what you do in secret, will reward you."[14]

There is a story about a man who stood up in synagogue one day and announced, "I wish to pledge $10,000—anonymously!" Well, good for him. Jesus, however, encourages giving so that the recipients have no idea who the giver is. It is all too easy to give as a way of stroking our own egos. Disentangling our motives for giving is difficult; being truly anonymous makes that easier.

14. Matthew 6:1-4.

> "What credit is it to you if you lend only to those who you expect will pay you back? Even sinners lend to each other, expecting to be repaid in full. But love your enemies, do good, and lend expecting nothing back! Your reward will be great, and you will be children of *Ha'Elyon* [the Most High]; for he is kind to the ungrateful and the wicked.[15]

Was there a side glance here at the famous rabbi Hillel's legislation called *prosbul*, which we looked at in chapter 1? Recall that Hillel encouraged loans by stipulating how they could be repaid even in the sabbatical year; Jesus, in encouraging loaning without the expectation of payback, may well have relied on moral suasion to accomplish the same goal. And perhaps he intended to go even further than the biblical law: seventh year or no seventh year, when you loan, do so as though the loan were a gift.

> Give, and you will receive gifts—the full measure, compacted, shaken together and overflowing, will be put right in your lap. For the measure with which you measure out will be used to measure back to you!"[16]

You have probably seen food containers marked, "Bag has been packed by weight, not by volume. Contents may have settled during shipping and handling." I suppose that is meant to settle your outrage when you notice that your box of pretzels looks half empty. Jesus implies that tzedakah works in the opposite way than packing wares for sale. He uses the image of a grain container. The grain is first poured in; then it's shaken to compress the grain into as small a volume as possible; and then, even more is put in, until the container is so full that the grain spills out. The idea is a basic one: you reap what you sow, you get out what you put in. Jesus, though, seems to be implying more: that for his followers, God will reward giving.

---

15. Luke 6:34-35.
16. Luke 6:38.

Sunday the Rabbi Read Leviticus

As background to the next story, let's look for a moment at the Talmud, which relates a comment made by Rabbi Isaac.[17] As rabbis were wont to do, he observed something unusual in the Hebrew text of Leviticus 2:1. Leviticus is the third book of the Bible and among other things, it details the kinds of sacrificial offerings that people made in ancient Israel.

Leviticus, by the way, was the first book that a Jewish child traditionally learned and he was given a treat of honey along with his first exposure to the biblical text. The modern reader opening the Bible for the first time will require more than honey to make it through Leviticus. While Genesis and the first half of Exodus, the first two books of the Bible, delight in giving us stories and characters we can relate to, Leviticus is full of priests, animals, blood and sacrifices and is sometimes approached like the third *Matrix* movie, the sequel that never should have been made. It also happens to be the book that tells us that the greatest commandment is to love God and the second greatest is to love our neighbor. But the bulls, goats and chickens tend to push that to one side. It may help to think of Leviticus as "The Artichoke of the Bible." It takes time to peel off the outer leaves and reach to the delicious heart, but any artichoke lover knows that it's worth it.

Back to Rabbi Isaac. Reading Leviticus 2:1, he observed—most likely without the aid of honey—that this is the only verse in the first few chapters of Leviticus that uses the word *nefesh*, or "soul." Literally it reads, "When a soul presents an offering of meal to the LORD, his offering shall be of choice flour." *Soul* really means a *person*: when a *person* brings an offering, just as we say, "Old King Cole was a merry old soul" to mean that the king was a person, a human being. But Rabbi Isaac was an ancient

17. The Talmud dates from several centuries after the time of Jesus, so is not really "background." But many of its traditions, and certainly its ethical values, go back much earlier. The story about R. Isaac is found in *b. Menachot* 104b.

word detective and he took the use of the word "soul" to point to something deeper. He opined that since most offerings of meal, or grain—as opposed to those of animals—were brought by poor people, the lesson is that God counts the offering of the poor as though they had offered their own souls—their very lives. In other words, concluded Rabbi Isaac, it costs the poor much more than the rich when they offer of their own sustenance.

And that brings us to a story about Jesus, in which the theme of care for widows overlaps that of tzedakah, showing that sometimes Jewish values are not easily separated.

The Lady and the Tzedakah Box

Tradition reports that in the first century there were thirteen boxes in the part of the Temple known as the "Court of the Women." (This was not an area exclusively for women, but the part beyond which women could not go.) Here, people of both genders could put gifts earmarked for the Temple into these ancient equivalents of thirteen tzedakah boxes. At the scene, Jesus has words for those who mistreat widows:

> As he taught them, he said, "Watch out for the kind of *Torah*-teachers who like to walk around in robes and be greeted deferentially in the marketplaces, who like to have the best seats in the synagogues and take the places of honor at banquets, who like to swallow up widows' houses while making a show of *davvening* [praying] at great length. Their punishment will be all the worse!"[18]

Judaism had structures in place to help the unfortunate and care for widows was certainly part of the Jewish value system. But then as now, there were always some individuals who were corrupt or greedy. Values express an ideal and life on the ground does not always match that ideal.

18. Mark 12:38-40. See also the parallel in Luke 20:45-47.

Here, the problem seems to have been that certain individuals—or perhaps the collective "establishment" of the time—were eating up the financial resources of many widows. Possibly the powers-that-be were levying excessive monetary tithes on them. Religious tithing, in which a portion of your income was given over to the Temple, was a requirement in first-century Judaism, a kind of ancient income tax. Some people, just as some modern politicians do, appear to have added additional tax burdens that ended up "swallowing up" the possessions of poor widows—not unlike the situation that Elisha addressed in 2 Kings 4.

In contrast to such actions which contravened the Jewish value system, Jesus commended a particular widow. Her name is not given, so we can call her Mrs. Moskovich. The passage continues:

> Then Yeshua sat down opposite the Temple treasury and watched the crowd as they put money into the offering-boxes. Many rich people put in large sums, but a poor widow came and put in two small coins.
>
> He called his *talmidim* to him and said to them, "Yes! I tell you, this poor widow has put more in the offering-box than all the others making donations. For all of them, out of their wealth, have contributed money they can easily spare; but she, out of her poverty, has given everything she had to live on."[19]

Jesus' comment here reminds us of Rabbi Isaac's view of the gifts of the poor (or maybe vice-versa since Rabbi Isaac lived later). Mrs. Moskovich here exemplifies another Jewish value, that of giving tzedakah. In this story, she has just sacrificially given to the Temple, which to a person of faith was in effect giving to God. The first-century Temple establishment was viewed as corrupt; perhaps the widow was somewhat naïve, or simply trusting God that the funds would be used appropriately. In any event, there is a subtext here: while certain people were robbing widows of their

19. Mark 12:41-44. See also the parallel in Luke 21:1-4.

livelihoods, God could be expected to vindicate Mrs. Moskovich for her humble and sacrificial attitude in giving tzedakah. What people were pulling down, God would build back up.

Jesus' followers continued to stress tzedakah, as these examples show:

> No one among them [the early community of Jesus' followers] was poor, since those who owned lands or houses sold them and turned over the proceeds to the emissaries [i.e., the apostles] to distribute to each according to his need.[20]
>
> I may give away everything that I own, I may even hand over my body to be burned; but if I lack love, I gain nothing.[21]
>
> So, having perceived what grace had been given to me, Ya'akov, Kefa and Yochanan [James, Peter and John], the acknowledged pillars of the community, extended to me and Bar-Nabba [Barnabas] the right hand of fellowship; so that we might go to the Gentiles, and they to the Circumcised. Their only request was that we should remember the poor—which very thing I have spared no pains to do.[22]

There might not have been blue boxes in the first century but had there been, Jesus, the poor widow and the apostle Paul would probably have been the first to put something in.

---

20. Acts 4:34-35.

21. 1 Corinthians 13:3; Paul in his well-known chapter on love. Again, attitude is important; grudging giving may in fact help the recipient, but it is not giving that is calculated to foster a mindset of tzedakah.

22. Galatians 2:9-10.

CHAPTER 8

THE DAY JESUS DID *Tikkun Olam*

The Bad Grandson

For all the healings and feedings that Jesus did, the New Testament focuses on one day in particular that Jesus did tikkun olam.

The life of Jesus is written in four gospels; *gospel* means "good news." The same word is found in the Hebrew Bible as *besorah*, carrying the same meaning. Interestingly, fully 20 to 30% of the text in the gospel accounts focuses on the last week of Jesus' life when he was put to death by crucifixion.[1] If there is good news in the story of Jesus, it seems odd to focus that much on the events that led up to his death. It would rather seem that books called "good news" would spend much more time on his teaching, or his healing, or his feeding, or anything other than his death—at least if you view Jesus as a "good guy," which the gospel writers certainly did.

Yet something odd is afoot in the story of Jesus. Churches around the world refer to the day on which Jesus died as "Good Friday," which adds yet another layer to the conundrum.[2] What

1. Leland Ryken, James C. Wilhoit, Tremper Longman III, eds., *Dictionary of Biblical Imagery* (Downers Grove, Ill.: InterVarsity Press, 1998), p. 626.
2. Assuming it was a Friday, the most common view; others think he died on a Wednesday or a Thursday.

exactly is "good" about dying on a cross, which was the common and rather gruesome Roman method of execution? Jewish history has its own records of crucifixion and those are most definitely *not* good. The following true story is rated PG-17.

About 90 B.C.E., Alexander Jannaeus (or Yannai) was the king of the Jewish people and a grandson of one of the Maccabees, the heroes of the Hanukkah story. Jannaeus was also the High Priest, which was supposed to be a separate office from king under a "checks and balances" policy that was earlier outlined in the Bible. Jannaeus' dual position was as though the President of the United States had arrogated to himself the position of Chief Justice of the Supreme Court. Unlike his grandfather and great-uncles the Maccabees, Jannaeus was no hero in the eyes of the Jews. Known for his ruthless oppression, he managed to provoke a civil war and to cause a group of Pharisees to revolt against his rule some 90 years before Jesus appeared on the scene.

The straw that broke the camel's back was this: among the various groups comprising the Jewish people of that time, the two main ones were the Sadducees—who were elitists, priests and in control of the Temple—and the Pharisees—who were teachers and populists. In other words, the one-percenters and the rest of us.

One Sukkot holiday, Jannaeus was in the Temple in Jerusalem. Among other festivities of the week, a "water show" took place which was one of the main highlights. Jannaeus, officiating as High Priest, was supposed to perform a ceremony that involved pouring water on the altar, Pharisee-style (even though the Sadducees controlled the Temple and everything that went on there, they knew the popular power of the Pharisees and often went along with the latter's idea of how to do things.) Instead, in a gesture of contempt for the Pharisees, he poured out the water on his feet. In response, the crowd started pelting Jannaeus with their *etrogs*, the citrons that are used on Sukkot along with the *lulavs*.[3] If Sukkot

3. Yes, technically the Hebrew should be *etrogim* and *lulavim*, but many Jews are not that particular.

was anything like it is today, you were supposed to wave the lulav and hold, not throw, the etrog. Getting hit with hundreds, perhaps thousands, of etrogs was not calculated to put Jannaeus in a good mood and in retaliation, he killed 6,000 of his fellow Jews in the courtyard of the Temple. Lovely.

Over the ensuing six years, the people were divided by civil war. The capstone, such as it was, came when Jannaeus, not content with his previous massacre of 6,000, crucified 800 Pharisees and slashed the throats of their wives and children while they were watching—all while he was eating and drinking during his evening soirée. So infamous was this horror, that as late as the 17th century C.E., the Dutch illustrator Willem Swidde made an engraving titled, "The Execution of the Pharisees by Alexander Jannaeus."[4] Whatever day of the week that happened, it was anything but good for the Jews.

So, Jews knew full well that crucifixion would not bode anyone well. Why, then, should the day Jesus was crucified be called "good"? As it turns out, according to the New Testament (I here paraphrase) it could as well have been called "Tikkun Olam Friday." Let me explain why.

The Math of Jesus: When 613 Equaled 2

What does a person have to do in order to be doing tikkun olam? Traditional Jews will direct us to the 613 mitzvot in the Torah, as interpreted by later rabbis. Others will point to specific activities that Jews and non-Jews alike can engage in to help "repair the world."

For Jesus, when it came to tikkun olam, loving God and loving people was his foundation and it was programmatic for him. There is a New Testament story that tells of a Pharisee who approached Jesus as people often did with their teachers:

4. See, e.g., www.antikforever.com/Syrie-Palestine/Hebreux-Israel-Juda/Images/hasmoneen12b.jpg. The image is often reproduced online; this is the largest instance I could find.

> And one of them who was a *Torah* expert asked a *sh'eilah* [question] to trap him: "Rabbi, which of the *mitzvot* in the *Torah* is the most important?" He told him, "'**You are to love the *ADONAI* your God with all your heart and with all your soul and with all your strength.**' This is the greatest and most important *mitzvah*. And a second is similar to it, '**You are to love your neighbor as yourself.**' All of the *Torah* and the Prophets are dependent on these two *mitzvot*."[5]

There are 613 commandments in the Law according to the traditional enumeration. How does one pick out the greatest from 613? Hillel the Great, living in the century before Jesus, offered to teach the entire Torah to a man while he stood on one foot. His lesson? "What is hateful to you, do not do to another. The rest is commentary. Go and learn." (Hillel's "evil twin," so to speak, the strict and harsh Shammai, reportedly beat the same man away with a stick.) And in the centuries following Jesus, one rabbi taught that Moses gave Israel 613 commandments, but David reduced them to eleven. Then Isaiah did him one better and boiled them down to two. Finally, according to the same rabbi, the prophet Habakkuk distilled all 613 to one commandment: "the righteous man is rewarded with life for his fidelity." Or as it often translated, "the righteous shall live by his faith."[6]

In keeping with this long-standing Jewish way of thinking, Jesus also reduced the 613 to the two commandments to love God and to love one's neighbor. The whole Torah and the Prophets too—in other words, the entire Bible[7]—is based on these twin commandments as their foundation, said Jesus. And the rest, as Hillel said, is commentary. I imagine Jesus and Hillel would have

---

5. Matthew 22:35-40. Boldface original.
6. Habakkuk 2:4; *b. Makkot* 23b–24a.
7. There is a third section called the "Writings," but this was Jesus' shorthand for the whole Scripture.

found a lot to talk about had they somehow been able to sit down together in a first-century Starbucks.[8]

Without of course using the phrase tikkun olam, the gospel accounts frequently offer observations like these:

> Yeshua went all over the Galil [Galilee] teaching in their synagogues, proclaiming the Good News of the Kingdom, and healing people from every kind of disease and sickness.[9]

> Yeshua went about all the towns and villages, teaching in their synagogues, proclaiming the Good News of the Kingdom, and healing every kind of disease and weakness.[10]

> [Jesus to his disciples] "Heal the sick, raise the dead, cleanse those afflicted with *tzara'at* [skin disease], expel demons. You have received without paying, so give without asking payment.[11]

> And large crowds came to him, bringing with them the lame, the blind, the crippled, the mute and many others. They laid them at his feet, and he healed them.[12]

In these instances, Jesus' acts of tikkun olam involve both healing from physical and spiritual ("drive out demons") afflictions. Interestingly, in some of the verses just quoted teaching and preaching are included in the same breath; words and learning can also do a lot to better the world.

The sort of acts of tikkun olam that were important to Jesus extended beyond healing and teaching to addressing the needs of the hungry, the imprisoned and the impoverished. At one point, he

---

8. Hillel died in 10 C.E., when Jesus would have been around 13 years old.
9. Matthew 4:23.
10. Matthew 9:35.
11. Matthew 10:8.
12. Matthew 15:30.

explains that such actions towards others[13] become acts of tikkun olam to him as well:

> "For I was hungry and you gave me food, I was thirsty and you gave me something to drink, I was a stranger and you made me your guest, I needed clothes and you provided them, I was sick and you took care of me, I was in prison and you visited me."[14]

Other writings of the New Testament encouraged Jesus' followers to do likewise. Just substitute "do acts of tikkun olam" for the italicized phrases:

> Therefore, as the opportunity arises, let us *do what is good* to everyone, and especially to the family of those who are trustingly faithful.[15]

> For we are of God's making, created in union with the Messiah Yeshua for *a life of good actions* already prepared by God for us to do.[16]

> As for those who do have riches in this present world, charge them not to be proud and not to let their hopes rest on the uncertainties of riches but to rest their hopes on God, who richly provides us with all things for our enjoyment. Charge them to *do good, to be rich in good deeds, to be generous and ready to share*.[17]

---

13. Bible scholars debate whether in context Jesus means acts toward people in general or acts towards his followers who are serving as his representatives. Either way, elsewhere the New Testament encourages acts of tikkun olam towards all people.

14. Matthew 25:35–36.

15. Paul to the congregation in Galatia, somewhere in modern Turkey; Galatians 6:10. Those bothered by the "especially to…" part should consult Ze'ev Maghren's book *John Lennon and the Jews: A Philosophical Rampage* (New Milford, CT: The Toby Press, 2014), in which he argues that real love is always preferential, as shown in the book of Deuteronomy and in real life.

16. Paul again to the congregation in Ephesus, also in modern Turkey; Ephesians 2:10.

17. Paul to his protégé Timothy; 1 Timothy 6:17-18. Some debate if Paul or someone else was actually the author of this book; that is immaterial to this discussion.

> But don't forget *doing good and sharing with others*, for with such **sacrifices** God is well pleased.[18]
>
> So let those who are suffering according to God's will entrust themselves to a faithful Creator by continuing to *do what is good.*[19]
>
> Suppose a brother or sister is without clothes and daily food, and someone says to him, "*Shalom*! Keep warm and eat hearty!" *without giving him what he needs*, what good does it do? Thus, faith by itself, unaccompanied by actions, is dead.[20]

Clearly tikkun olam was part of the essence of New Testament teaching.

"Lady, You Got a Problem"

When I was a kid, *Mad* magazine, then all the vogue in the eleven-to-twelve-year old circuit, ran a cartoon about not Superman but "Super-Man," the superintendent of an apartment building likely somewhere in New York City. The "super," plunger in hand, enters an apartment where the tenant, a middle-aged, heavy-set woman, is loudly calling for him while water rapidly pours in from an unknown location, already up to her waist and rising fast. The super sizes up the situation for a moment and then in the sort of understatement that caring yet hardened New Yorkers are capable of, tells her, "Lady—you got a problem." Indeed.

The universe and human life have problems. Things *are* broken, hence the need of "repairing" them.[21] But this raises an obvious question: Why is the world in need of repair in the first place?

---

18. An unknown author to a community of Jewish followers of Jesus; Hebrews 13:16. Boldface original.
19. Peter to a persecuted community of Jesus-followers; 1 Peter 4:19.
20. James 2:15–17.
21. If you doubt this, this would be a good time to break out Bob Dylan's album *Oh Mercy* and listen to the song "Everything Is Broken."

Remember Isaac Luria, the 16th-century rabbi and mystic whom we met in chapter 1? His version of the kabbalah brought the phrase tikkun olam into widespread currency, and Luria attributed the entrance of evil into the world to the breaking of cosmic jars and the descent of divine sparks to earth. Yet neither the Hebrew Bible nor the New Testament talk about jars and sparks. The brokenness of life is traced in the Bible to humanity itself, not to something that happened "out there," such as the "breaking of the shells." The Bible uncomfortably puts more emphasis on our own responsibility for sin and evil as well as less stock in our ability to set things right.

Some years ago, there was a popular comic strip, *Pogo*, in which humanoid opossums, turtles and other inhabitants of Okefenokee Swamp lampooned the political affairs of the day. In perhaps inadvertent agreement with the Bible, the strip's creator Walt Kelly had Pogo saying, "We have met the enemy and he is us" (a phrase apparently earlier used during Earth Day of 1970 and parodying Commodore Oliver Perry's remark during the War of 1812, "We have met the enemy and they are ours"). The phrase retains currency, as the web site Humor in America notes: "It is still used in public discourse to describe, for instance, the potential results of man-made global warming. And cartoonist Jim Morin paraphrased it in a poignant drawing following the murders of servicemen at Ft. Hood in April of 2014."[22]

Walt Kelly's observation about the source of evil is reinforced by an incident from the late 1920s. At that time there was a highly publicized trial, involving Ruth Snyder and Judd Gray, both accused of the murder of Snyder's husband Albert. The trial was widely, if not obsessively, covered in the newspapers, not least because Ruth Snyder was young and the mother of a little girl. Both parties were convicted and sentenced to die by the

---

22. Larry Bush, "The Morphology of a Humorous Phrase: 'We have met the enemy and he is us'," humorinamerica.wordpress.com/2014/05/19/the-morphology-of-a-humorous-phrase/

electric chair. Concerning Snyder and Gray, historian Donald L. Miller observed:

> It was their "lack of distinction" wrote Alexander Woollcott, that held people's attention. "They were just average folk—the ordinary suburban people in moderate circumstances that you jostle every day in Grand Central, the Pennsylvania station, or on the Jersey ferries," the News editorialized. "Ruth was a rather good-looking housewife in the editor's modest home in Queens Village. Albert Snyder . . . liked to sit around the house evenings, with a pipe and a book... It might have been the household of your next-door neighbor."
>
> Judd Gray was "equally obscure and average. He was a traveling salesman, a church member, a lodge man and known as a good father and husband in East Orange." If these seemingly normal suburbanites could commit such a ghastly crime, nearly anyone could.[23]

The observation that humanity can be its own worst enemy has suggested to many that there is a radical nature to human evil. This is illustrated, for example, in the biblical book of Ecclesiastes (also known as Kohelet[24]), in which the author observes: "For there is not one good man on earth who does what is best and doesn't err."[25] This translation, taken from the JPS version, may tread too lightly; the final word implies "missing the mark," namely the mark of God's standards. Or in other words, "sinning."

The author of Ecclesiastes was not alone. Jeremiah has God saying that,

> My people are stupid,
> They give Me no heed;

23. Donald L. Miller, *Supreme City: How Jazz Age Manhattan Gave Birth to Modern America* (New York: Simon & Schuster, 2014), pp. 366-67.

24. *Kohelet*, or *Qohelet*, is the name of the book in Hebrew, often translated as "Preacher."

25. Ecclesiastes 7:20.

> They are foolish children,
> They are not intelligent.
> They are clever at doing wrong,
> But unable to do right.[26]

In three rapid metaphors, Jeremiah sizes up the people: they are *stupid*, usually translated as "foolish," which you will recall, refers to people who don't have their act together, who can't cut it in life, who lack the right stuff because they ignore God and what he has to say about life.

Not only that, they are *foolish children* who know nothing and haven't yet developed sense, ill-equipped for the challenges of life, still learning right from wrong. Yet quite unlike young children, they are *clever at doing wrong*; they have honed their "skills" in doing the wrong thing. Fools, toddlers and practiced criminals. Or as it is worded even more strongly in Jeremiah 13:23: "Can the Cushite change his skin, Or the leopard his spots? Just as much can you do good, Who are practiced in doing evil!" A similar observation, in starker terms, was made by atheist Christopher Hitchens (whose mother was Jewish). Profoundly affected by the events of 9/11, he described them as "simply evil."[27]

Judaism traditionally has painted a picture of humanity as able to choose equally between good and evil. Yet this leaves us wondering why evil then seems so pervasive. I once described the biblical picture of evil and sin in the following way. No doubt people do many good and beautiful things, from creating art to finding more humane forms of existence through social action or legislation. But consider a single human being. When, God forbid, something like cancer strikes, we don't say, "Yes, but think about the parts of them that are well." Rather (at least if we are fighters) we attack the cancer vigorously and try to root it out. The "good parts" and the cancer are *not* equal players. Cancer is an invasion

26. Jeremiah 4:22.

27. Larry Taunton, *The Faith of Christopher Hitchens: The Restless Soul of the World's Most Notorious Atheist* (Nashville, TN: Nelson Books, 2016), p. 71.

of a healthy body. Sin and evil, like cancer, are invasions into the body of humanity which was created in God's image.

What Kind of Tikkun Olam Can Heal Our World?

With such a radical problem, what is the solution—if there even is one? One time I watched a television reporter interview a "typical" person on the street about something whose details I no longer recall. Whatever the issue under discussion was, Ms. Typical Citizen said that, "Someone should do something about it." The reporter pressed her: "What should they do?" Ms. T.C. answered plaintively, "I don't know. But *something*." I hope that was not typical of the body politic at large. But it underscores how easy it is to recognize a problem, how much harder to figure out the solution.

Animal Planet

If you have attended synagogue services, you may know that there are several services each day: the morning service, called *Shacharit*; the afternoon service, called *Minchah*; and the evening service, or *Ma'ariv*. On the Sabbath and holidays, there is also the additional, or *Musaf*, service. The morning and afternoon services were intentionally established to correspond with the morning and afternoon sacrifices of animals that took place each day in the Jerusalem Temple prior to its destruction in 70 C.E. The Musaf service corresponds to the additional sacrifices made on Sabbaths and holidays. (The evening service is different; it derives from the traditional obligation to recite the Shema in the evening.)

The fact that Jews used to sacrifice animals needs a bit of explaining—and yes, this does have to do with the topic of tikkun olam. Before 70 C.E., Jews routinely sacrificed bulls, goats, rams and other animals as the means of atoning for sin. Many Jews no longer think much about sin except on Yom Kippur, but in the first century and before, sacrificing animals was a year-round activity for Jews. Realize that you committed a sin, winter, spring, summer or fall—all you had to do was call on God and offer a sacrifice, along with a repentant heart.

The idea seems to be that the animal suffered punishment and went to death in place of the worshipper, who otherwise would have consequences to face. This didn't let anyone off the hook as far as sinning against other people was concerned—if you stole Uncle Morey's favorite Jerry Garcia tie, there was still restitution to be made, or a fine to be paid. The sacrifices did, however, procure forgiveness for sinning against God when accompanied by repentance, which is to say, when done with a proper heart motive and not simply as an unthinking mechanical act. Only with the destruction of the Temple and the loss of the entire sacrificial system did the rabbis institute means of atonement that did not include sacrifice: repentance alone, or along with fasting and doing tzedakah.[28]

The sacrifices were therefore another way that tikkun olam was done in the Hebrew Bible. While various acts of kindness and proactive advocacy for justice and righteousness helped better the world, the sacrifices addressed the root level of the problem—the pervasiveness of sin and its effects.

The Day Jesus Did Tikkun Olam

As we have seen, Jesus distilled the 613 commandments of the Torah into two: to love God and to love others. Just as the animal sacrifices helped bring about tikkun olam in ancient Israel, the New Testament invites its readers to understand that Jesus' death was also a means of tikkun olam, for it was the ultimate example of loving others. It was done to better the world, by offering atonement for sin and reconciliation with God, and in a deeper way than the ancient sacrifices could. The animals had no idea why they were being killed, but Jesus voluntarily gave up his life for others: "No one has greater love than a person who lays

28. There were also sacrifices that were offered for different reasons, such as giving thanks for deliverance from a difficult situation.

down his life for his friends,"[29] he said in reference to his own impending death.

Recall chapter 3, where we talked about the Jewish value of kiddush haShem. That phrase sometimes referred to martyrdom, when Jewish people would give up their lives rather than convert. We can broaden the idea of martyrdom to include, for example, someone sacrificing their life to benefit others—in wartime, for example, in order to save a buddy. This would certainly be an act of tikkun olam, an example of loving others more than one's self. To reiterate a New Testament passage quoted in that chapter, "Now it is a rare event when someone gives up his life even for the sake of somebody righteous, although possibly for a truly good person one might have the courage to die. But God demonstrates his own love for us in that the Messiah died on our behalf while we were still sinners."[30] Kiddush haShem, loving others, atoning for our sin—this is why the day Jesus was crucified is known as *Good* Friday.

For atonement and reconciliation with God betters the lives of anyone who experiences them. That in turn allows us to most fully reconcile with other people, with the environment and with ourselves. Individually and societally, we lay the foundation for a better world.

Jesus said as much when two of his disciples were jockeying for power:

> Ya'akov and Yochanan [James and John], the sons of Zavdai [Zebedee], came up to him and said, "Rabbi, we would like you to do us a favor." He said to them, "What do you want me to do for you?" They replied, "When you are in your glory, let us sit with you, one on your right and the other on your left."[31]

29. John 15:13.
30. Romans 5:7-8.
31. Mark 10:35-37.

In other words: "When you, Jesus, bring in the Kingdom of God, make one of us the Secretary of State and the other one your National Security Advisor. We want to meet with you every day and have complete access and walk in the corridors of power." Long story short, Jesus had this to say:

> But Yeshua called them to him and said to them, "You know that among the *Goyim*, those who are supposed to rule them become tyrants, and their superiors become dictators. But among you, it must not be like that! On the contrary, whoever among you wants to be a leader must be your servant; and whoever wants to be first among you must become everyone's slave! For the Son of Man did not come to be served, but to serve—and to give his life as a ransom for many."[32]

Using a title by which he frequently referred to himself, "Son of Man,"[33] Jesus intimates that he would demonstrate the nature of real service by giving up his life for the benefit of others. He describes his death as a "ransom," a word that in the biblical world suggested the idea of atonement: as the sacrificed animals "ransomed" the worshipper from the consequences of sin, Jesus' death would also be sacrificial and atoning.

Jesus' made the same point more explicitly at his final Passover seder, which has come to be known as "the Last Supper":[34]

> Also he took a cup of wine, made the *b'rakhah* [blessing], and gave it to them, saying, "All of you, drink from it! For this is my blood, which ratifies the New Covenant, my

32. Mark 10:42-45.

33. Long story short, the title "Son of Man" goes back to Daniel 7 where it represented a divine yet human figure who would rule in God's kingdom. By using this title instead of simply saying, "I," Jesus linked what he was all about to the Hebrew scriptures and their teaching.

34. The modern Passover seder is more developed than it was in the first century, and it is probably anachronistic to even call Jesus' Passover meal a "seder." "Proto-seder" might be more accurate. But it had bitter herbs and cups of wine, even if no charoset or haggadah. Some scholars debate whether it was a Passover meal at all, but that is the presentation that the New Testament gives us, and Passover provides the context and meaning for what Jesus said.

> blood shed on behalf of many, so that they may have their sins forgiven.[35]

This was not your grandfather's seder and probably not yours either. Jesus took what today is the third of the four cups, said the *borei pri hagafen* (or the first-century equivalent) and then said something you will not find in any haggadah. He referred to the wine as symbolizing his blood which "shed" in death would mean that people can "have their sins forgiven."

The only talk of blood at a modern seder would be if Cousin Maxie cut his finger and needed a Band-Aid, but first-century Jews were not squeamish about the subject. With sacrifices of animals happening constantly in the Temple, blood was a part of life. When Jesus connected his blood with the "forgiveness of sins," he was connecting with the world of first-century Judaism; he was being explicit that his death would be a means of atonement and therefore of tikkun olam.

The same thought is carried throughout the New Testament. One of Jesus' disciples, Peter, says that,

> God has exalted this man [Jesus] **at his right hand** as Ruler and Savior, in order to enable Isra'el to do *t'shuvah* [repentance] and have her sins forgiven.[36]

Paul visits the city of Pisidian Antioch where:

> … on *Shabbat* they went into the synagogue and sat down. After the reading from the *Torah* and from the Prophets, the synagogue leaders sent them a message, "Brothers, if any of you has a word of exhortation for the people, speak!"[37]

In an earlier chapter, I recalled that when the rabbi of my synagogue rose up to speak, others rose up too—namely, to take a

35. Matthew 26:27-28.
36. Acts 5:31. Boldface original.
37. Acts 13:14-15.

walk outside and light up a smoke. The rabbi ended up speaking to the committed core who were either polite or genuinely interested in the rabbi's thoughts. At Pisidian Antioch, though, rabbis as we know them today didn't yet exist, and so why shouldn't everyone hear from a visitor who after all might have something new to say? And Paul indeed did have something new to offer. After a rather long speech, he tells the gathered congregation concerning Jesus:

> "Therefore, brothers, let it be known to you that through this man is proclaimed forgiveness of sins!"[38]

The response:

> As they left, the people invited Paul and Bar-Nabba [Barnabas] to tell them more about these matters the following *Shabbat*.[39]

Apparently, the idea that Jesus' death could bring about forgiveness of sins and atonement was seriously considered by the congregation. (At other times, more vigorous debate and even opposition occurred, but the point here is that Jesus' death could easily be understood by first-century Jews in the context of sacrifice and atonement.)

And so the day that commemorates Jesus' death by crucifixion is called "Good Friday." His death was understood to procure forgiveness from sins, atonement and tikkun olam. The world begins to be repaired when *we* are repaired. In turn, we become the kind of people who can extend God's tikkun olam to the rest of the world.

May tikkun olam, and great shalom, overflow our hurting world!

38. Acts 13:38.
39. Acts 13:42.

EPILOGUE

It's a joke older than Methuselah, but I like this version better than any other I've seen:

A man is rescued from a desert island after 20 years. The news media, amazed at this feat of survival, ask him to show them his home.

"How did you survive? How did you keep sane?" they ask him, as he shows them around the small island.

"I had my faith. My faith as a Jew kept me strong. Come." He leads them to a small glen, where stands an opulent temple, made entirely from palm fronds, coconut shells and woven grass. The news cameras take pictures of everything—even a *torah* made from banana leaves and written in octopus ink. "This took me five years to complete."

"Amazing! And what did you do for the next fifteen years?"

"Come with me." He leads them around to the far side of the island. There, in a shady grove, is an even *more* beautiful temple. "This one took me twelve years to complete!"

"But sir" asks the reporter, "Why did you build *two* temples?"

"This is the temple *I* attend. That other place? Hah! I wouldn't set foot in that other temple if you PAID me!"[1]

1. "Jewish Humour," en.wikipedia.org/wiki/Jewish_humour

Sometimes, though, truth is stranger than fiction, or than old jokes. At one time—true story—Bermuda had 110 Jews and two synagogues. The second synagogue broke away from the first because they could not agree on how much Hebrew to use in the service. Or maybe that was a pretext for splitting over personality clashes between the rabbis. In any event, one of the rabbis was eventually deported, resulting in a net loss of one shul.[2]

It's the one that's not there in Bermuda anymore that *I* wouldn't set foot in. Because I can't.

We Jews are great at differing. Years ago, the esteemed author Abba Hillel Silver wrote a book called *Where Judaism Differed* to explain how he understood Judaism to be distinct from Christianity (and other ancient forms of belief). He should only have written *Where* Jews *Differed*. He would have had enough for three volumes: Reform, Orthodox, too much Hebrew, not enough Hebrew, the rabbi is paid too much, the rabbi is paid too little, the sukkah is too big, the sukkah is too small, more jelly apples for kids on Simchat Torah, fewer jelly apples, "you want their teeth to rot?"… and on and on.

Yet amazingly, amid this cacophony of opinions and disagreements, Jewish values stand as unshakeable non-negotiables of Jewish life. What Jew will argue against honoring one's parents? Who ever heard of Jews *not* in favor of giving tzedakah? Whoever cheered for something that *wasn't* good for the Jews? What Jews argue that gossip is a *good* thing (even if we practice it ourselves)? If you happen to be Jewish and believe in dishonoring your father, hoarding money for yourself alone, or hoping that things will be bad for the Jews—well, you are a very small minority and you may want to consider setting up that second shul for yourself.

2. Joe Pranevich, "Old News—Proof to the Joke that a Jew on a Tropical Island Would Build Two Synagogues," www.coatofmanycolors.net/2012/08/25/old-news-proof-to-the-joke-that-a-jew-on-a-tropical-island-would-build-two-synagogues/

For the rest of us, though we may differ on the details, we know and we try to honor the core values that have helped shape us as a people over the millennia.

What many of us haven't known is that Jesus and the New Testament have also been part of this ancient stream of living out and passing on our values, which values, as I've tried to show, go back to the Hebrew Bible and (what I believe, at any rate) to God himself.

Jesus and his Jewish followers in the first century attempted to embody these values in their lives. Each value would only be perfectly lived out when complete tikkun olam would come to the world. For when the world would be repaired, all parents everywhere would be honored, everything would be good for the Jews (and the non-Jews too), tzedakah would no longer be needed and all speech would be uplifting, helpful and truthful.

And as we've seen, Jesus' followers believe that one day above all others was the day that began this process—the day that Jesus died on a Roman execution stake and atoned for sin—the day Jesus *especially* did tikkun olam.

Tikkun Olam Friday. That was some day!

GLOSSARY

Most of these terms are defined in the book as they come up. Here they are conveniently gathered in one place, should you forget the definitions as you read along.

Adonai — "Lord," used in place of saying the sacred name of God. The sacred name is often also rendered as "the Lord."

Al Chet — "for the sin," the name of prayer on Yom Kippur (the Day of Atonement), enumerating a variety of sins for which we ask forgiveness.

Aliyah — "going up," used to mean the act of immigrating to Israel. Also used of the honor in synagogue services in which certain individuals are invited to "go up" and recite the prescribed blessings over Scripture.

Almanah, pl. *almanot* — a widow

Ashkenazi(c) — referring to Jews of Eastern European and German origin. One reads about both Ashkenazi Jews and Ashkenazic Jews; either term is acceptable. Compare *Sephardi(c)*, *Mizrachi* below.

B'rakhah (or *berakhah, bracha*, etc.) — a blessing, usually one that is prescribed in Judaism for a particular occasion.

Besorah — the term in the Hebrew Bible for "news" or especially, "good news." The equivalent of "gospel," which in the Greek New Testament means "good news."

Borei pri hagafen — "who creates the fruit of the vine," the blessing recited over wine at the Friday evening *kiddush* (sanctification) ceremony opening the Sabbath, at Passover, and on other occasions.

Bris — the ritual of circumcision.

Charoset — a mixture of fruit and spices used at Passover. It reminds us of the mortar used in the building projects the Hebrew slaves were forced to work on. It may also remind us of the sweetness of God's redemption.

Chillul Hashem — "desecration of the Name," in which "the Name" refers to God. Any act which reflects poorly on God and poorly on God's people, the Jews. The opposite of *kiddush haShem* (for which see below).

Daven — or, *davven*. To pray.

Dayenu — "enough for us," a song sung at Passover that declares that God has done more than was necessary for the Jewish people in redeeming us from Egypt and giving us the Torah.

Dibbah — a report, or a bad report.

Ein Sof — literally, "without end," the name for God in the Kabbalah as "he is in himself," as it is often expressed. But God cannot be directly known as he is in himself, but (in the Kabbalah) through the ten *sefirot* (which see below).

Emet — truth.

Etrog — a citron used ceremonially during the Feast of Tabernacles, or *Sukkot*.

Ferkakte — variously spelled. A Yiddish adjective meaning ridiculous, crazy, "damn" — in other words, referring to something the speaker finds distasteful, annoying, or worse.

Get, pl. *gittin* — a certificate of divorce, required under religious Jewish law for a divorce to take place.

Golem — a creature in kabbalistic lore, made of clay and brought to life when the Hebrew word *emet* (truth) is inscribed on its forehead. Removing the first letter of *emet* produces the word *met*, dead, and turns the golem back to inanimate clay.

Gonif — a thief.

Goyim — Gentiles, non-Jews.

Haftarah — the weekly synagogue reading that corresponds to the Torah reading for that week. Usually from the historical books or the prophets, it relates thematically or in some other way to the content of the Torah reading.

Haggadah, pl. *haggadot* — literally, "telling" or "story." The book that guides participants through a Passover *seder* (for which see below). There are thousands of *haggadot* (or *haggadahs*, if you are not particular about the correct plural form) differing in layout, artistic treatment, and interpretive comments, though all follow the same basic outline.

HaShem — "the Name," used by religious Jews to refer to God.

Haskhnasat Orchim — extending hospitality

Kabbalah — literally, "that which is received," referring to Jewish mystical traditions which originated in the Middle Ages, and sometimes even earlier.

Kefa — the Hebrew name for the New Testament character Peter. This was the "nickname" given to Simon, one of the apostles, by Jesus. *Kefa* is Aramaic for "rock" (and is often rendered as "Cephas" in English translations). *Peter* is Greek for the same thing.

Kibbud Av va'Em — showing honor to one's father and mother.

Kiddush Hashem — "sanctification of the Name," in which "the Name" refers to God. Any act which reflects well on God and well on God's people, the Jews, because it accomplishes God's will in the world. The opposite of *chillul haShem* (for which see above).

Kippah — a skullcap worn by religious Jews and sometimes by others as a mark of Jewish identity. *Kippah* is Hebrew; the Yiddish equivalent is *yarmulka*.

Kohen — a priest. Today someone can know if they are of a priestly family only through family tradition; there are no genealogical records that go back that far.

Lashon — the tongue; or, a language.

Lashon Hara — basically, "evil speech," especially gossip. In this book I use the term of encompass other kinds of evil speech besides gossip, though technically there are separate terms for those.

Lulav — an assemblage of palm branches, willow leaves, and myrtle leaves used ceremonially during the Feast of Tabernacles, or *Sukkot*. As put together, it resembles a vegetative light saber.

Ma'ariv — the evening synagogue service.

Maot Hittim (or *Maot Hittin*) — literally, "wheat money," referring to the provision of money or food at Passover time to those too poor to be able to afford matzah or other Passover provisions.

Maror — the bitter herbs used at Passover, prescribed in Exodus 12:8 and Numbers 9:11.

Matzah — unleavened bread, prescribed for Passover in Exodus 12:8 and Numbers 9:11.

Minchah — the afternoon synagogue service.

Mitzvah, pl. *mitzvot* — a commandment. There are 613 biblical *mitzvot* in the Bible; there are also others which are later, rabbinic commandments.

Mizrachi — literally, "eastern," an adjective referring to Jews from the areas of Iran and Iraq, and sometimes from North Africa and other areas as well. Compare *Ashkanazi(c)* above and *Sephardi(c)* below.

Musaf — the "additional" synagogue service on Shabbat and holidays, usually added to the *Shacharit* service (for which see below).

Nefesh — soul, or a living person.

Nudnik — someone who just won't stop pestering and bothering you.

Pesach — the Hebrew word for Passover.

Pidyon ha-Ben — a ceremony, usually performed on the 31st day after a male child is born, by which he is "redeemed" (see Exodus 13:13-16). This is done by paying five silver coins to a *kohen*, or priest.

Plotz — to faint or collapse, as from horror. Generally used humorously.

Prosbul — a legal convention created by Rabbi Hillel the Great. It allowed for the collection of loans every seventh year; for details, see chapter 1.

Pushke — a box used to collect money for *tzedakah*, or charity.

Ra — "evil," part of the expression *lashon hara.*

Raca — An Aramaic insult meaning "empty headed" or "moron"

Rakhil — a slanderer

Sabra — someone native-born in the Land of Israel. The term originates from the prickly pear (*tzabar* in Hebrew), tough on the outside but sweet on the inside. This is supposed to be reflective of Israeli character traits.

Seder — the ceremonial service today held on the first two nights of Passover in the Diaspora and on the first night only in Israel. Jesus' "Last Supper" was a Passover meal[1] and a sort of proto-seder, as the modern seder did not fully develop until some time later.

Sefirah, pl. *sefirot* — in the kabbalah, ten "emanations" or ways in which God in himself (the *Ein Sof*, for which see above) interacts and relates with the world of creation.

Sephardi(c) — referring to Jews of Spanish and Portuguese descent, and those from the European countries along the Mediterranean. Compare *Ashkenazi(c)* and *Mizrachi* above.

Shabbat — the weekly Sabbath.

Shacharit — the morning synagogue service.

Shalom — Hebrew for "peace," and used as a greeting when coming and when going.

Shema — pronounced "sh'mah." The cardinal prayer of Judaism, consisting of Deuteronomy 6:4-9, Deuteronomy 11:13-21 and Numbers 15:37-41. The name of prayer is taken from Deuteronomy 6:4, *Shema Yisrael, Adonai Elohenu, Adonai echad*, "Hear O Israel, the LORD our God, the LORD is One."

1. That it was a Passover meal is disputed by some scholars, but represents my position.

Shevirat kelim — In the kabbalah, the "breaking of the vessels" whereby divine sparks fell to earth, bringing evil into the created world. By performing the *mitzvot* (see *mitzvah* above), we can according to kabbalah raise the sparks back to God and perform tikkun olam.

Sukkah – the booth used during *Sukkot*, or the Feast of Tabernacle. Religious Jews will live or at least take their meals in the *sukkah* for the week of the holiday.

Taka — or, *take* or *takeh*. Yiddish for "really," with the implication, "Wouldn't you really think that…?"

Talmid — a disciple, a student of a rabbi.

Tanakh — the Hebrew Bible, or Old Testament, or First Testament, depending on your term of choice. The word is an acronym for the three parts of the Hebrew Bible: *T*orah (Five Books of Moses); *N*evi'im (Prophets, including many of the historical books); and *K*etuvim (Writings, the remainder of the books).

T'shuvah — or, *teshuvah*. Repentance.

Tikkun Olam — literally, "repair of the world." For details, see this entire book.

Torah — the Five Books of Moses, also referred to in English as the Pentateuch. Every synagogue has a hand-written scroll of the Torah kept in an ark. The word can also mean "teaching," that is, divine teaching, in general.

Tuchus — a person's bottom or rear. Used humorously.

Tzedakah — charity.

Tzimtzum — in kabbalah, God's "contraction" of himself, enabling the creation of the universe.

Yenta — a busybody or gossip, especially referring to a woman.

Yeshua — Jesus' name in Hebrew (or Aramaic). It means something like, "God saves."

Yetom, pl. *yetomim* — an orphan.

Zohar — the 13th-century "textbook" or main text of the kabbalah. Its name means "splendor."

Bibliography

Abramowitz, Jack. *Kibud Av'V'eim*. NCSY Torah on One Foot Series; New York: National Conference of Synagogue Youth, n.d. www.ou.org/torah/attachment/33983

Abramowitz, Jack. *Tzedaka*. NCSY Torah on One Foot Series; New York: National Conference of Synagogue Youth, n.d. https://slideblast.com/queue/tzedaka_59afca0f1723dde08755e23d.html

Adlerstein, Yitzchok. "What's Wrong with Us?" cross-currents.com/2009/10/21/whats-wrong-with-us/

"Americans Know Big Macs Better than Ten Commandments." www.reuters.com/article/2007/10/12/us-bible-commandments-idUSN1223894020071012

"The Anne Frank Center USA Proudly Presents 'Lashon Hara: On the Consequences of Hate Speech'," www.prweb.com/releases/2014/11/prweb12336281.htm

Ausubel, Nathan. *A Treasury of Jewish Folklore: Stories, Traditions, Legends, Humor, Wisdom and Folk Songs of the Jewish People.* New York: Crown, 1948.

Ballela, David. "The Site of the Israel Orphan Asylum." knickerbockervillage.blogspot.com/2008/12/site-of-israel-orphan-asylum.html

"Bernard Madoff." en.wikipedia.org/wiki/Bernard_Madoff

"Black and White No Lashon Hara Graphic T-Shirt." www.zazzle.com/black_and_white_no_lashon_hara_graphic_t_shirt-235649431772680225

Bush, Larry. "The Morphology of a Humorous Phrase: 'We have met the enemy and he is us'." humorinamerica.wordpress.com/2014/05/19/the-morphology-of-a-humorous-phrase/

Crowley, Carolyn Hughes. "Meet Me at the Automat." www.smithsonianmag.com/arts-culture/meet-me-at-the-automat-47804151/

"Defining the Bystander Effect: Kitty Genovese Murder & Research by Latane and Darley." study.com/academy/lesson/defining-the-bystander-effect-kitty-genovese-murder-research-by-latane-and-darley.html

Donahue, John R. and Daniel J. Harrington, *The Gospel of Mark*. Collegeville, MN: The Liturgical Press, 2005.

Dylan, Bob. "Everything Is Broken." *Oh, Mercy!* [album]. Columbia Records CK-45281, 1989.

Eisenberg, Ronald L. *The JPS Guide to Jwish Traditions*. Philadelphia: Jewish Publication Society, 2004.

Fishman, Sylvia Barack. *The Way into the Varieties of Jewishness*. Woodstock, VT: Jewish Lights Publishing, 2007.

Forchheimer, Elliot. "Does It Really Matter How I Drive?" www.myjewishlearning.com/texts/Bible/Weekly_Torah_Portion/emor_ujafedny5761.shtml

France, R. T. *The Gospel of Matthew*. Grand Rapids, MI/Cambridge, UK, 2007.

"Free Yenta iPhone App Finds Jewish Dates by Location." www.jewishhumorcentral.com/2012/10/free-yenta-iphone-app-finds-jewish.html

Gerace, Alyssa. "Exploring Senior Living Niches: Jewish Retirement Communities." bitly.com/retirecom

Gross, Jane. *A Bittersweet Season: Caring for Our Aging Parents—and Ourselves*. New York: Alfred A. Knopf, 2011.

Gutow, Steve. "A Seder Lesson: Let All Who Are Hungry Come And Eat." www.huffingtonpost.com/rabbi-steve-gutow/let-all-who-are-hungry-co_b_520203.html

"A History of the Charity Box." www.chabad.org/library/article_cdo/aid/390485/jewish/A-History-of-the-Charity-Box.htm

Hoffman, Matthew. *From Rebel to Rabbi: Reclaiming Jesus and the Making of Modern Jewish Culture*. Stanford, Stanford University Press, 2007.

"Hospitality: Look Who's Coming for Dinner!" www.chabad.org/library/article_cdo/aid/691769/jewish/Hospitality.htm

[International Beis Horaah Din newsletter]. www.dinonline.org/wp-content/uploads/newsletter/en_106.pdf

"(Is It) Good for the Jews?" [podcast]. www.isitgoodforthejews.com/about/

Isaacs, Ronald H. "Maot Hittin: Wheat Money." www.myjewishlearning.com/article/maot-hittin-wheat-money/

J. Correspondent [Jonathan Rubin], "Honor Thy Mother, Even If Shes [*sic*] a Meddler." www.jweekly.com/article/full/29210/honor-thy-mother-even-if-she-s-a-meddler

"Janusz Korczak (1878–1942)." www.jewishvirtuallibrary.org/janusz-korczak

"Jewish Humour." en.wikipedia.org/wiki/Jewish_humour

"JNF's Iconic Blue Box Redesigned." usa.jnf.org/about-jnf/jnfs-iconic-blue-box-1.html

Jones, Robert P. and Daniel Cox. *Chosen for What? Jewish Values in 2012: Findings from the 2012 Jewish Values Survey*. Washington, DC: Public Religion Research Institute, Inc., 2012. www.prri.org/research/jewish-values-in-2012/

Joselit, Jenna Weissman. "When Pushke Came to Shove." www.forward.com/culture/14464/when-pushke-came-to-shove-02738/

Keener, Craig S., *The IVP Bible Background Commentary: New Testament*. Downers Grove, IL: InterVarsity Press, 1993.

Klug, Lisa Alcalay. "Top Ten Jewish Neighborhoods." lisaklug.com/articles-2/arts-culture/jewish-living-magazine-cover-story/

Lederman, Amy Hirshberg. "Honor Your Parents—And Believe in Them." www.azjewishpost.com/2010/honor-your-parents-—-and-believe-in-them/

Leibovitz, Liel. "'Lashon Hara': Available Now on a Phone Near You." www.tabletmag.com/jewish-arts-and-culture/162932/lashon-hara-secret-app

Maghren, Ze'ev. *John Lennon and the Jews: A Philosophical Rampage*. New Milford, CT: The Toby Press, 2014.

Mark, Jonathan. "Jeremy Balkin, 31." www.thejewishweek.com/special-sections/36-under-36/tikkun-olam-wall-street-jeremy-balkin-31

Miller, Donald L. *Supreme City: How Jazz Age Manhattan Gave Birth to Modern America*. New York: Simon & Schuster, 2014.

Mogel, Wendy. "Honoring Guests," www.kveller.com/article/honoring-guests/

Pranevich, Joe. "Old News—Proof to the Joke that a Jew on a Tropical Island Would Build Two Synagogues." www.coatofmanycolors.net/2012/08/25/old-news-proof-to-the-joke-that-a-jew-on-a-tropical-island-would-build-two-synagogues/

"Rent-A-Yenta House Cleaning Service." www.facebook.com/Rent-A-Yenta-House-Cleaning-Service-136821933033118/

Rosenberg, Yair. "Yale President Calls on Graduates to Commit to Tikkun Olam." www.tabletmag.com/scroll/191120/yale-president-peter-salovey-calls-on-graduates-to-commit-to-tikkun-olam

Ryken, Leland; James C. Wilhoit; and Tremper Longman III, eds., *Dictionary of Biblical Imagery*. Downers Grove, Ill.: InterVarsity Press, 1998.

"Seinfeld Monologues." laughbreak.com/quotes/seinfeld-monologues/

Sholkoff, Avi. "Hachnasat Orchim: What a Jewish Value Can Teach Us About the Syrian Refugee Crisis." www.huffingtonpost.com/avi-sholkoff/hachnasat-orchim_b_8587164.html

Shukert, Rachel. "Rabbi Stephen Sondheim." www.tabletmag.com/scroll/169206/rabbi-stephen-sondheim

Sichel, Ilana. "The Ancient Belief in Jewish Bones Tunneling to Jerusalem on Judgment Day." thejewniverse.com/2016/the-ancient-belief-in-jewish-bones-tunneling-to-jerusalem-on-judgment-day/

Smith, Melanie B. "Can You Name All 10?" legacy.decaturdaily.com/decaturdaily/religion/071027/ten.shtml

Solny, Shiryn. "Christian Supermodel Miranda Kerr Says She Keeps Mystical Jewish Text in Her Handbag for a 'Little Protection'." www.algemeiner.com/2016/08/04/christian-supermodel-miranda-kerr-keeps-mystical-jewish-text-in-her-handbag-for-a-little-protection-video/

Solny, Shiryn. "New Video Shows Israelis Thanking Shanghai for Sheltering Jewish WWII Refugees." www.algemeiner.com/2015/08/28/new-video-shows-israelis-thanking-shanghai-for-sheltering-jewish-wwii-refugees/

Swidde, Willem. "The Execution of the Pharisees by Alexander Jannaeus" [engraving]. www.antikforever.com/Syrie-Palestine/Hebreux-Israel-Juda/Images/hasmoneen12b.jpg

"Tahara Supplies for the Chevra Kadisha." www.jewish-funerals.org/tahara-supplies-chevra-kadisha

Taunton, Larry. *The Faith of Christopher Hitchens: The Restless Soul of the World's Most Notorious Atheist*. Nashville, TN: Nelson Books, 2016.

Telushkin, Joseph. *Jewish Literacy: The Most Important Things to Know About the Jewish Religion, Its People and Its History*. New York: William Morrow, 1991.

"Tikkun Olam." templeisaiah.com/tikkun-olam.php

UJA Federation New York web site. www.ujafedny.org

Walton, John H.; Victor Harold Matthews; and Mark W. Chavalas. *The IVP Bible Background Commentary: Old Testament*. Downers Grove, Ill.: InterVarsity Press, 2000.

"Widows & Orphans—Mishpatim." bitly.com/widows-orphans

Witherington, Ben. *The Gospel of Mark: A Socio-rhetorical Commentary*. Grand Rapids, MI: Eerdmans, 2001.

"Yenta." www.merriam-webster.com/dictionary/yenta

"Yentl." www.avotaynu.com/books/yentl.htm

Other Related Resources

Available at Messianic Jewish Resources Int'l. • www.messianicjewish.net
1-800-410-7367
(Check our website for current discounts and promotions)

First Time in History!

General Editor: Rabbi Barry Rubin
Theological Editor: Dr. John Fischer

< Hardcover Edition

The Complete Jewish Study Bible

Insights for Jews and Christians

—Dr. David H. Stern

A One-of-a-Kind Study Bible that illuminates the Jewish background and context of God's word so it is more fully understandable. Uses the updated *Complete Jewish Bible* text by David H. Stern, including notes from the *Jewish New Testament Commentary* and contributions from Scholars listed below. 1990 pages.

Hardback	978-1619708679	$49.95
Flexisoft	978-1619708693	$79.95
Leather	978-1619708709	$139.95

Leather Edition w/color gift box   Flexisoft Edition w/color sleeve

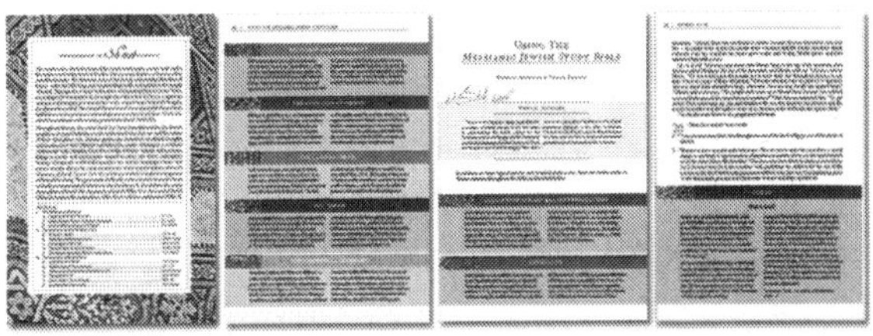

CONTRIBUTORS & SCHOLARS

Rabbi Dr. Glenn Blank
Dr. Michael Brown
Rabbi Steven Bernstein
Rabbi Joshua Brumbach
Rabbi Ron Corbett
Pastor Ralph Finley
Rabbi Dr. John Fischer
Dr. Patrice Fischer
Rebbitzen Malkah Forbes
Rabbi Dr. David Friedman
Dr. Arnold Fruchtenbaum
Dr. John Garr
Pastor David Harris
Benjamin Juster
Rabbi Dr. Daniel Juster
Dr. Walter C. Kaiser
Rabbi Barney Kasdan
Dr. Craig S. Keener
Rabbi Elliot Klayman
Jordan Gayle Levy
Dr. Ronald Moseley
Rabbi Dr. Rich Nichol
Rabbi Mark J. Rantz
Rabbi Russ Resnik
Dr. Richard Robinson
Rabbi Dr. Jacob Rosenberg
Rabbi Isaac Roussel
Dr. Michael Rydelnik
Dr. Jeffrey Seif
Rabbi Tzahi Shapira
Dr. David H. Stern
Dr. Bruce Stokes
Dr. Tom Tribelhorn
Dr. Forrest Weiland
Dr. Marvin Wilson

QUOTES BY JEWISH SCHOLARS & SAGES

Dr. Daniel Boyarin
Dr. Amy-Jill Levine
Rabbi Jonathan Sacks
Rabbi Gamaliel
Rabbi Hillel
Rabbi Shammai
Rabbi Akiva
Maimonides
and many more

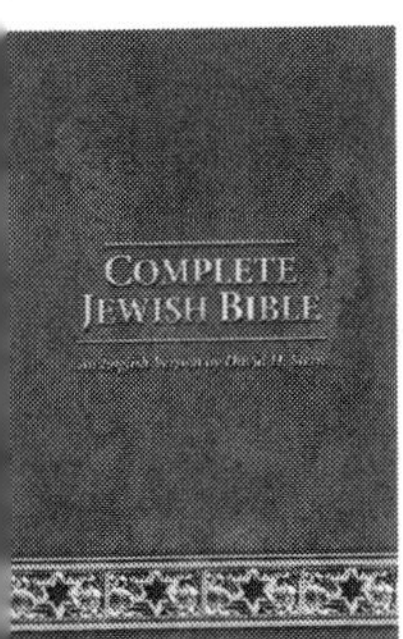

Complete Jewish Bible: *An English Version*

—Dr. David H. Stern (Available March 2017)

Now, the most widely used Messianic Jewish Bible around the world, has updated text with introductions added to each book, written from a biblically Jewish perspective. The CJB is a unified Jewish book, a version for Jews and non-Jews alike; to connect Jews with the Jewishness of the Messiah, and non-Jews with their Jewish roots. Names and terms are returned to their original Hebrew and presented in easy-to-understand transliterations, enabling the reader to say them the way *Yeshua* (Jesus) did! 1728 pages.

Paperback	978-1936716845	$29.95
Hardcover	978-1936716852	$34.95
Flexisoft Cover	978-1936716869	$49.95

Jewish New Testament

—Dr. David H. Stern

The New Testament is a Jewish book, written by Jews, initially for Jews. Its central figure was a Jew. His followers were all Jews; yet no other version really communicates its original, essential Jewishness. Uses neutral terms and Hebrew names. Highlights Jewish references and corrects mistranslations. Freshly translated into English from Greek, this is a must read to learn about first-century faith. 436 pages

Hardback	978-9653590069	**JB02**	$19.99
Paperback	978-9653590038	**JB01**	$14.99
Spanish	978-1936716272	**JB17**	$24.99

Also available in French, German, Polish, Portuguese and Russian.

Jewish New Testament Commentary

—Dr. David H. Stern

This companion to the *Jewish New Testament* enhances Bible study. Passages and expressions are explained in their original cultural context. 15 years of research. 960 pages.

Hardback	978-9653590083	**JB06**	$34.99
Paperback	978-9653590113	**JB10**	$29.99

A Life of Favor

A Family Therapist Examines the Story of Joseph and His Brothers

—Rabbi Russell Resnik, MA, LPCC

Favor is an inherent part of God's reality as Father, and properly understood is a source of blessing to those who want to know him. The story of Jacob's sons points to a life of favor that can make a difference in our lives today.

Excellent insight—judgments in exegesis are matched by skillful use of counseling principles and creative applications to contemporary situations in life and in the family. —Walter C. Kaiser, Jr. President Emeritus, Gordon-Conwell Theological Seminary, Hamilton, Mass. 212 Pages

Paperback	978-1936716913	$19.99

Will the Nazi Eagle Rise Again?

What the Church Needs to Know about BDS and Other Forces of Anti-Semitism

–David Friedman, Ph.D.

This is the right book at the right time. exposing the roots of Anti-Semitism being resurrected in our days, especially in our Christian Church.
—Dr. Hans-Jörg Kagi, Teacher, Theologian, Basle, Switzerland

Timely and important response to the dangerous hatred of the State of Israel that is growing in society and in the Church.
—Michael Rydelnik, Prof. of Jewish Studies, Moody Bible Inst., Chicago, Ill.

Israel is not an apartheid state and bears absolutely no resemblance to the institutionalized racial oppression that I lived under in South Africa. I am deeply offended by this comparison.
—Luba Mayekiso, Africa for Israel Christian Coalition, Republic of South Africa

Paperback (278 Pages) 978-1936716876 $19.99

The Day Jesus Did Tikkun Olam

—Richard A. Robinson, Ph.D.

Easy-to-read, yet scholarly, explores ancient Jewish and Christian scriptures, relevant stories and biblical parallels, to explain the most significant Jewish value—*tikkun olam*—making this world a better place. This is a tenet of both religions, central to the person of Jesus himself.
—Murray Tilles, Director, Light of Messiah Ministries; M.Div.

A wealth of scholarship and contemporary relevance with great insight into Jewish ethics and the teachings of Jesus.
—Dr. Richard Harvey, Senior Researcher, Jews for Jesus

146 pages	978-1-936716-98-2	$ 18.99

Zipporah's Farm

—Written by Ani Perez, Illustrated by Deborah Wilson

I believe animals are a gift that God has given to us for our pleasure. They should be loved and protected. They are innocent and never should be killed for sport. I welcome you to my farm, where there is an abundance of love, peace and joy. It is a place where anyone at any age can escape into fantasy and forget about the world's troubles, even if only for a little while. Welcome to Zipporah's Farm.
Large 8.5 x 11 inches, 60 pages, with full color illustrations.

Hardcover	978-1-936716-97-5	$24.99
Paperback	978-1-936716-96-8	$19.99

The Book of Ruth

This delightful version of *The Book of Ruth* includes the full text from the *Complete Jewish Bible* on the left page of the two-page spread. On the right are artful illustrations with brief story summaries that can be read to young children. Can be read any time during the year, but especially on *Shavuot* (Pentecost), the anniversary of the giving of the Torah on Mount Sinai and when the Holy Spirit was poured out on Yeshua's disciples (Acts 2). *The Book of Ruth* points to Yeshua as the ultimate Kinsman Redeemer.
6 x 9 inches, 26 pages with full color illustrations.

978-1-936716-94-4	$ 9.99

The Book of Esther

This delightful version of *The Book of Esther* includes the full text from the *Complete Jewish Bible* on the left page of the two-page spread. On the right are artful illustrations with brief story summaries that can be read to young children. Can be read any time during the year, but especially during *Purim*, the festival that celebrates how Queen Esther risked her life and became a vessel for the deliverance of her people Israel. Though God is not mentioned, Mordecai and Esther humbled themselves before God by fasting and praying, which showed dependence upon him. God answered and delivered his people while bringing the proud Haman to justice.
6 x 9 inches, 34 pages with full color illustrations.

978-1-936716-95-1	$ 9.99

Jewish Giftedness & World Redemption

The Calling of Israel

—Jim Melnick

All things are mortal but the Jew; all other forces pass, but he remains. What is the secret of his immortality?

—Mark Twain, Concerning the Jews, *Harper's Magazine*, September, 1899.

The most comprehensive research of the unique achievements of the Jewish people. The author comes up with the only reason that makes sense of this mystery.

—Daniel C. Juster, Th.D., Restoration from Zion of Tikkun International

Paperback (280 Pages) 978-1-936716-88-3 $24.99

Messianic Judaism *A Modern Movement With an Ancient Past*

—David H. Stern

An updated discussion of the history, ideology, theology and program for Messianic Judaism. A challenge to both Jews and non-Jews who honor Yeshua to catch the vision of Messianic Judaism. 312 pages

978-1880226339 **LB62** $17.99

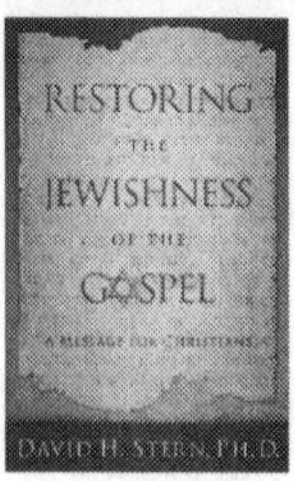

Restoring the Jewishness of the Gospel

A Message for Christians

—David H. Stern

Introduces Christians to the Jewish roots of their faith, challenges some conventional ideas, and raises some neglected questions: How are both the Jews and "the Church" God's people? Is the Law of Moses in force today? Filled with insight! Endorsed by Dr. Darrell L. Bock. 110 pages

English	978-1880226667	**LB70**	$9.99
Spanish	978-9653590175	**JB14**	$9.99

The Return of the Kosher Pig *The Divine Messiah in Jewish Thought*

—Rabbi Tzahi Shapira

The subject of Messiah fills many pages of rabbinic writings. Hidden in those pages is a little known concept that the Messiah has the same authority given to God. Based on the Scriptures and traditional rabbinic writings, this book shows the deity of Yeshua from a new perspective. You will see that the rabbis of old expected the Messiah to be divine. Softcover, 352 pages.

"One of the most interesting and learned tomes I have ever read. Contained within its pages is much with which I agree, some with which I disagree and much about which I never thought. Rabbi Shapria's remarkable book cannot be ignored."

—Dr. Paige Patterson, President, Southwest Baptist Theological Seminary

978-1936716456 **LB81** $ 39.99

Proverbial Wisdom & Common Sense

A Messianic Commentary

—Derek Leman

A Messianic Jewish Approach to Today's Issues from the Proverbs
A devotional style commentary, divided into chapters suitable for daily reading. An encyclopedia of practical advice on topics relevant to everyone. 248 pages

Paperback 978-1880226780 **LB98** $19.99

Matthew Presents Yeshua, King Messiah *A Messianic Commentary*

—Rabbi Barney Kasdan

Few commentators are able to truly present Yeshua in his Jewish context. Most don't understand his background, his family, even his religion, and consequently really don't understand who he truly is. This commentator is well versed with first-century Jewish practices and thought, as well as the historical and cultural setting of the day, and the 'traditions of the Elders' that Yeshua so often spoke about. Get to know Yeshua, the King, through the writing of another rabbi, Barney Kasdan. 448 pages

978-1936716265 **LB76** $29.99

Rabbi Paul Enlightens the Ephesians on Walking with Messiah Yeshua

A Messianic Commentary

—Rabbi Barney Kasdan

The Ephesian were a diverse group of Jews and Gentiles, united together in Messiah. They definitely had an impact on the first century world in which they lived. But the Rabbi was not just writing to that local group. What is Paul saying to us? 160 pages.

Paperback 978-11936716821 **LB99** $17.99

James the Just Presents Application of Torah

A Messianic Commentary

—Dr. David Friedman

James (Jacob) one of the Epistles written to first century Jewish followers of Yeshua. Dr. David Friedman, a former Professor of the Israel Bible Institute has shed new light for Christians from this very important letter.

978-1936716449 **LB82** $14.99

Jude On Faith and the Destructive Influence of Heresy

A Messianic Commentary

—Rabbi Joshua Brumbach

Almost no other canonical book has been as neglected and overlooked as the Epistle of Jude. This little book may be small, but it has a big message that is even more relevant today as when it was originally written.

978-1-936716-78-4 **LB97** $14.99

Psalms & Proverbs *Tehillim* תְּהִלִּים-*Mishlei* מִשְׁלֵי

—Translated by Dr. David Stern

Contemplate the power in these words anytime, anywhere: Psalms-*Tehillim* offers uplifting words of praise and gratitude, keeping us focused with the right attitude; Proverbs-*Mishlei* gives us the wisdom for daily living, renewing our minds by leading us to examine our actions, to discern good from evil, and to decide freely to do the good. Makes a wonderful and meaningful gift. Softcover, 224 pages.

978-1936716692 LB90 $9.99

At the Feet of Rabbi Gamaliel

Rabbinic Influence in Paul's Teachings

—David Friedman, Ph.D.

Paul (Shaul) was on the "fast track" to becoming a sage and Sanhedrin judge, describing himself as passionate for the Torah and the traditions of the fathers, typical for an aspiring Pharisee: "…trained at the feet of Gamaliel in every detail of the Torah of our forefathers. I was a zealot for God, as all of you are today" (Acts 22.3, CJB). Did Shaul's teachings reflect Rabbi Gamaliel's instructions? Did Paul continue to value the Torah and Pharisaic tradition? Did Paul create a 'New' Theology? The results of the research within these pages and its conclusion may surprise you. Softcover, 100 pages.

978-1936716753 **LB95** $8.99

Debranding God *Revealing His True Essence*

—Eduardo Stein

The process of 'debranding' God is to remove all the labels and fads that prompt us to understand him as a supplier and ourselves as the most demanding of customers. Changing our perception of God also changes our perception of ourselves. In knowing who we are in relationship to God, we discover his, and our, true essence. Softcover, 252 pages.

978-1936716708 **LB91** $16.99

Under the Fig Tree *Messianic Thought Through the Hebrew Calendar*

—Patrick Gabriel Lumbroso

Take a daily devotional journey into the Word of God through the Hebrew Calendar and the Biblical Feasts. Learn deeper meaning of the Scriptures through Hebraic thought. Beautifully written and a source for inspiration to draw closer to Adonai every day. Softcover, 407 pages.

978-1936716760 **LB96** $25.99

Under the Vine *Messianic Thought Through the Hebrew Calendar*

—Patrick Gabriel Lumbroso

Journey daily through the Hebrew Calendar and Biblical Feasts into the B'rit Hadashah (New Testament) Scriptures as they are put in their rightful context, bringing Judaism alive in it's full beauty. Messianic faith was the motor and what gave substance to Abraham's new beliefs, hope to Job, trust to Isaac, vision to Jacob, resilience to Joseph, courage to David, wisdom to Solomon, knowledge to Daniel, and divine Messianic authority to Yeshua. Softcover, 412 pages.

978-1936716654 **LB87** $25.99

Come and Worship *Ways to Worship from the Hebrew Scriptures*

—Compiled by Barbara D. Malda

We were created to worship. God has graciously given us many ways to express our praise to him. Each way fits a different situation or moment in life, yet all are intended to bring honor and glory to him. When we believe that he is who he says he is [see *His Names are Wonderful!*] and that his Word is true, worship flows naturally from our hearts to his. Softcover, 128 pages.

978-1936716678 **LB88** $9.99

His Names Are Wonderful

Getting to Know God Through His Hebrew Names

—Elizabeth L. Vander Meulen and Barbara D. Malda

In Hebrew thought, names did more than identify people; they revealed their nature. God's identity is expressed not in one name, but in many. This book will help readers know God better as they uncover the truths in his Hebrew names. 160 pages.

978-1880226308 **LB58** $9.99

The Revolt of Rabbi Morris Cohen

Exploring the Passion & Piety of a Modern-day Pharisee

—Anthony Cardinale

A brilliant school psychologist, Rabbi Morris Cohen went on a one-man strike to protest the systematic mislabeling of slow learning pupils as "Learning Disabled" (to extract special education money from the state). His disciplinary hearing, based on the transcript, is a hilarious read! This effusive, garrulous man with an irresistible sense of humor lost his job, but achieved a major historic victory causing the reform of the billion-dollar special education program. Enter into the mind of an eighth-generation Orthodox rabbi to see how he deals spiritually with the loss of everything, even the love of his children. This modern-day Pharisee discovered a trusted friend in the author (a born again believer in Jesus) with whom he could openly struggle over Rabbinic Judaism as well as the concept of Jesus (Yeshua) as Messiah. Softcover, 320 pages.

978-1936716722 **LB92** $19.99

Stories of Yeshua

—Jim Reimann, Illustrator Julia Filipone-Erez

Children's Bible Storybook with four stories about Yeshua (Jesus). *Yeshua is Born: The Bethlehem Story* based on Lk 1:26-35 & 2:1-20; *Yeshua and Nicodemus in Jerusalem* based on Jn 3:1-16; *Yeshua Loves the Little Children of the World* based on Matthew 18:1–6 & 19:13–15; *Yeshua is Alive-The Empty Tomb in Jerusalem* based on Matthew 26:17-56, Jn 19:16-20:18, Lk 24:50-53. Ages 3-7, Softcover, 48 pages.

978-1936716685 **LB89** $14.99

To the Ends of the Earth – How the First Jewish Followers of Yeshua Transformed the Ancient World

— Dr. Jeffrey Seif

Everyone knows that the first followers of Yeshua were Jews, and that Christianity was very Jewish for the first 50 to 100 years. It's a known fact that there were many congregations made up mostly of Jews, although the false perception today is, that in the second century they disappeared. Dr. Seif reveals the truth of what happened to them and how these early Messianic Jews influenced and transformed the behavior of the known world at that time.

978-1936716463 **LB83** $17.99

Jewish Roots and Foundations of the Scriptures I & II

—John Fischer, Th.D, Ph.D.

An outstanding evangelical leader once said: "There is something shallov about a Christianity that has lost its Jewish roots." A beautiful painting i a careful interweaving of a number of elements. Among other things, ther are the background, the foreground and the subject. Discovering the root of your faith is a little like appreciating the various parts of a painting. I the background is the panorama of preparation and pictures found in the Ol Testament. In the foreground is the landscape and light of the first centur Jewish setting. All of this is intricately connected with and highlights th subject—which becomes the flowering of all these aspects—the comin of God to earth and what that means for us. Discovering and appreciatin your roots in this way broadens, deepens and enriches your faith and you understanding of Scripture. This audio is 32 hours of live class instruction audio is clear and easy to understand.

9781936716623 **LCD03 / LCD04** $49.99 eac

The Gospels in their Jewish Context

—John Fischer, Th.D, Ph.D.

An examination of the Jewish background and nature of the Gospels in thei contemporary political, cultural and historical settings, emphasizing eac gospel's special literary presentation of Yeshua, and highlighting the cultura and religious contexts necessary for understanding each of the gospels. 3 hours of audio/video instruction on MP3-DVD and pdf of syllabus.

978-1936716241 **LCD01** $49.99

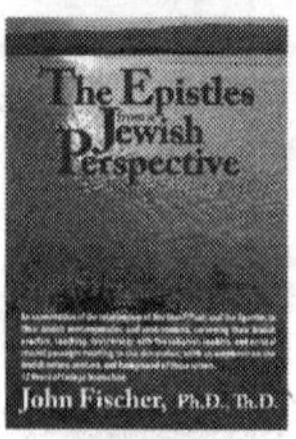

The Epistles from a Jewish Perspective

—John Fischer, Th.D, Ph.D.

An examination of the relationship of Rabbi Shaul (the Apostle Paul) an the Apostles to their Jewish contemporaries and environment; survey their Jewish practices, teaching, controversy with the religious leaders, an many critical passages, with emphasis on the Jewish nature, content, an background of these letters. 32 hours of audio/video instruction on MP3 DVD and pdf of syllabus.

978-1936716258 **LCD02** $49.99

The Red Heifer *A Jewish Cry for Messiah*

—Anthony Cardinale

Award-winning journalist and playwright Anthony Cardinale has travele extensively in Israel, and recounts here his interviews with Orthodo rabbis, secular Israelis, and Palestinian Arabs about the current search fo a red heifer by Jewish radicals wishing to rebuild the Temple and bring th Messiah. These real-life interviews are interwoven within an engaging an dramatic fictional portrayal of the diverse people of Israel and how the would react should that red heifer be found. Readers will find themselves i the Land, where they can hear learned rabbis and ordinary Israelis talkin about the red heifer and dealing with all the related issues and the imminen coming and identity of Messiah.

978-1936716470 LB79 $19.99

The Borough Park Papers

—Multiple Authors

As you read the New Testament, you "overhear" debates first-century Messianic Jews had about critical issues, e.g. Gentiles being "allowed" into the Messianic kingdom (Acts 15). Similarly, you're now invited to "listen in" as leading twenty-first century Messianic Jewish theologians discuss critical issues facing us today. Some ideas may not fit into your previously held pre-suppositions or pre-conceptions. Indeed, you may find some paradigm shifting in your thinking. We want to share the thoughts of these thinkers with you, our family in the Messiah.

Symposium I:

The Gospel and the Jewish People
248 pages

978-1936716593 LB84 $39.95

Symposium II:

The Deity of Messiah and the Mystery of God
211 pages

978-1936716609 LB85 $39.95

Symposium III:

How Jewish Should the Messianic Community Be?

978-1936716616 LB86 $39.95

Passion for Israel: *A Short History of the Evangelical Church's Support of Israel and the Jewish People*

—Dan Juster

History reveals a special commitment of Christians to the Jews as God's still elect people, but the terrible atrocities committed against the Jews by so-called Christians have overshadowed the many good deeds that have been performed. This important history needs to be told to help heal the wounds and to inspire more Christians to stand together in support of Israel.

978-1936716401 **LB78** $9.99

On The Way to Emmaus: *Searching the Messianic Prophecies*

—Dr. Jacques Doukhan

An outstanding compilation of the most critical Messianic prophecies by a renowned conservative Christian Scholar, drawing on material from the Bible, Rabbinic sources, Dead Sea Scrolls, and more.

978-1936716432 LB80 $14.99

Yeshua *A Guide to the Real Jesus and the Original Church*

—Dr. Ron Moseley

Opens up the history of the Jewish roots of the Christian faith. Illuminates the Jewish background of Yeshua and the Church and never flinches from showing "Jesus was a Jew, who was born, lived, and died, within first century Judaism." Explains idioms in the New Testament. Endorsed by Dr. Brad Young and Dr. Marvin Wilson. 213 pages.

978-1880226681 **LB29** $12.99

Gateways to Torah *Joining the Ancient Conversation on the Weekly Portion*

—Rabbi Russell Resnik

From before the days of Messiah until today, Jewish people have read from and discussed a prescribed portion of the Pentateuch each week. Now, a Messianic Jewish Rabbi, Russell Resnik, brings another perspective on the Torah, that of a Messianic Jew. 246 pages.

978-1880226889 **LB42** $15.99

Creation to Completion *A Guide to Life's Journey from the Five Books of Moses*

—Rabbi Russell Resnik

Endorsed by Coach Bill McCartney, Founder of Promise Keepers & Road to Jerusalem: "Paul urged Timothy to study the Scriptures (2 Tim. 3:16), advising him to apply its teachings to all aspects of his life. Since there was no New Testament then, this rabbi/apostle was convinced that his discipl[e] would profit from studying the Torah, the Five Books of Moses, and the Old Testament. Now, Rabbi Resnik has written a warm devotional commentary that will help you understand and apply the Law of Moses to your life in a practical way." 256 pages

978-1880226322 **LB61** $14.99

Walk Genesis! Walk Exodus! Walk Leviticus! Walk Numbers! Walk Deuteronomy!

Messianic Jewish Devotional Commentaries

—Jeffrey Enoch Feinberg, Ph.D.

Using the weekly synagogue readings, Dr. Jeffrey Feinberg has put together some very valuable material in his "Walk" series. Each section includes a short Hebrew lesson (for the non-Hebrew speaker), key concepts, an excellent overview of the portion, and some practical applications. Can be used as a daily devotional as well as a Bible study tool.

Walk Genesis!	238 pages	978-1880226759	**LB34**	$12.99
Walk Exodus!	224 pages	978-1880226872	**LB40**	$12.99
Walk Leviticus!	208 pages	978-1880226926	**LB45**	$12.99
Walk Numbers!	211 pages	978-1880226995	**LB48**	$12.99
Walk Deuteronomy!	231 pages	978-1880226186	**LB51**	$12.99
SPECIAL! Five-book Walk!		5 Book Set **Save $10**	**LK28**	$54.99

Good News According To Matthew

—Dr. Henry Einspruch

English translation with quotations from the Tanakh (Old Testament) capitalized and printed in Hebrew. Helpful notations are included. Lovely black and white illustrations throughout the book. 86 pages.

978-1880226025 **LB03** $4.99

Also available in Yiddish. **LB02** $4.99

They Loved the Torah *What Yeshua's First Followers Really Thought About the Law*

—Dr. David Friedman

Although many Jews believe that Paul taught against the Law, this book disproves that notion. An excellent case for his premise that all the first followers of the Messiah were not only Torah-observant, but also desired to spread their love for God's entire Word to the gentiles to whom they preached. 144 pages. Endorsed by Dr. David Stern, Ariel Berkowitz, Rabbi Dr. Stuart Dauermann & Dr. John Fischer.

978-1880226940 **LB47** $9.99

The Distortion *2000 Years of Misrepresenting the Relationship Between Jesus the Messiah and the Jewish People*

—Dr. John Fischer & Dr. Patrice Fischer

Did the Jews kill Jesus? Did they really reject him? With the rise of global anti–Semitism, it is important to understand what the Gospels teach about the relationship between Jewish people and their Messiah. 2000 years of distortion have made this difficult. Learn how the distortion began and continues to this day and what you can do to change it. 126 pages. Endorsed by Dr. Ruth Fleischer, Rabbi Russell Resnik, Dr. Daniel C. Juster, Dr. Michael Rydelnik.

978-1880226254 **LB54** $11.99

---

eBooks Now Available!

Versions available for your favorite reader

kindle nook Reader kobo

Visit www.messianicjewish.net for direct links to these readers for each available eBook.

God's Appointed Times *A Practical Guide to Understanding and Celebrating the Biblical Holidays* – **New Edition.**

—Rabbi Barney Kasdan

The Biblical Holy Days teach us about the nature of God and his plan fo mankind, and can be a source of God's blessing for all believers–Jew and Gentiles–today. Includes historical background, traditional Jewis observance, New Testament relevance, and prophetic significance, plu music, crafts and holiday recipes. 145 pages.

English	978-1880226353	**LB63**	$12.99
Spanish	978-1880226391	**LB59**	$12.99

God's Appointed Customs *A Messianic Jewish Guide to the Biblical Lifecycle and Lifestyle*

— Rabbi Barney Kasdan

Explains how biblical customs are often the missing key to unlockin the depths of Scripture. Discusses circumcision, the Jewish wedding, an many more customs mentioned in the New Testament. Companion to *God Appointed Times*. 170 pages.

English	978-1880226636	**LB26**	$12.99
Spanish	978-1880226551	**LB60**	$12.99

Celebrations of the Bible *A Messianic Children's Curriculum*

Did you know that each Old Testament feast or festival finds its fulfillmen in the New? They enrich the lives of people who experience and enjo them. Our popular curriculum for children is in a brand new, user-friendl format. The lay-flat at binding allows you to easily reproduce handout and worksheets. Celebrations of the Bible has been used by congregations Sunday schools, ministries, homeschoolers, and individuals to teac children about the biblical festivals. Each of these holidays are presented fo Preschool (2-K), Primary (Grades 1-3), Junior (Grades 4-6), and Children' Worship/Special Services. 208 pages.

978-1880226261 **LB55** $24.99

Passover: *The Key That Unlocks the Book of Revelation*

—Daniel C. Juster, Th.D.

Is there any more enigmatic book of the Bible than Revelation? Controvers concerning its meaning has surrounded it back to the first century. Toda the arguments continue. Yet, Dan Juster has given us the key that unlock the entire book—the events and circumstances of the Passover/Exodus. B interpreting Revelation through the lens of Exodus, Dan Juster provides unified overview that helps us read Revelation as it was always meant to b read, as a drama of spiritual conflict, deliverance, and above all, worshi He also shows how this final drama, fulfilled in Messiah, resonates with th Torah and all of God's Word. — Russ Resnik, Executive Director, Union o Messianic Jewish Congregations.

978-1936716210 **LB74** $10.99

The Messianic Passover Haggadah

Revised and Updated

—Rabbi Barry Rubin and Steffi Rubin.

Guides you through the traditional Passover seder dinner, step-by-step. Not only does this observance remind us of our rescue from Egyptian bondage, but, we remember Messiah's last supper, a Passover seder. The theme of redemption is seen throughout the evening. What's so unique about our Haggadah is the focus on Yeshua (Jesus) the Messiah and his teaching, especially on his last night in the upper room. 36 pages.

English	978-1880226292	**LB57**	$4.99
Spanish	978-1880226599	**LBSP01**	$4.99

The Messianic Passover Seder Preparation Guide

Includes recipes, blessings and songs. 19 pages.

English	978-1880226247	**LB10**	$2.99
Spanish	978-1880226728	**LBSP02**	$2.99

The Sabbath *Entering God's Rest*

—Barry Rubin & Steffi Rubin

Even if you've never celebrated Shabbat before, this book will guide you into the rest God has for all who would enter in—Jews and non-Jews. Contains prayers, music, recipes; in short, everything you need to enjoy the Sabbath, even how to observe havdalah, the closing ceremony of the Sabbath. Also discusses the Saturday or Sunday controversy. 48 pages.

978-1880226742 **LB32** $6.99

Havdalah *The Ceremony that Completes the Sabbath*

—Dr. Neal & Jamie Lash

The Sabbath ends with this short, yet equally sweet ceremony called havdalah (separation). This ceremony reminds us to be a light and a sweet fragrance in this world of darkness as we carry the peace, rest, joy and love of the Sabbath into the work week. 28 pages.

978-1880226605 **LB69** $4.99

Dedicate and Celebrate!

A Messianic Jewish Guide to Hanukkah

—Barry Rubin & Family

Hanukkah means "dedication" — a theme of significance for Jews and Christians. Discussing its historical background, its modern-day customs, deep meaning for all of God's people, this little book covers all the how-tos! Recipes, music, and prayers for lighting the menorah, all included! 32 pages.

978-1880226834 **LB36** $4.99

The Conversation

An Intimate Journal of the Emmaus Encounter

—Judy Salisbury

"Then beginning with Moses and with all the prophets, He explained t them the things concerning Himself in all the Scriptures." Luke 24:27
If you've ever wondered what that conversation must have been like, thi captivating book takes you there.
"The Conversation brings to life that famous encounter between the tw disciples and our Lord Jesus on the road to Emmaus. While it is based i part on an imaginative reconstruction, it is filled with the throbbing pulse o the excitement of the sensational impact that our Lord's resurrection shoul have on all of our lives." ~ Dr. Walter Kaiser President Emeritus Gordon Conwell Theological Seminary. Hardcover 120 pages.

Hardcover	978-1936716173	**LB73**	$14.99
Paperback	978-1936716364	**LB77**	$9.99

Growing to Maturity

A Messianic Jewish Discipleship Guide

—Daniel C. Juster, Th.D.

This discipleship series presents first steps of understanding and spiritua practice, tailored for the Jewish believer. It's purpose is to aid the believe in living according to Yeshua's will as a disciple, one who has learned th example of his teacher. The course is structured according to recent advance in individualized educational instruction. Discipleship is serious business an the material is geared for serious study and reflection. Each chapter is divide into short sections followed by study questions. 256 pages.

978-1936716227 **LB75** $19.99

Growing to Maturity Primer: *A Messianic Jewish Discipleship Workbook*

—Daniel C. Juster, Th.D.

A basic book of material in question and answer form. Usable by everyone 60 pages.

978-0961455507 **TB16** $7.99

Conveying Our Heritage A Messianic Jewish Guide to Home Practice

—Daniel C. Juster, Th.D. Patricia A. Juster

Throughout history the heritage of faith has been conveyed within th family and the congregation. The first institution in the Bible is the famil and only the family can raise children with an adequate appreciation of ou faith and heritage. This guide exists to help families learn how to pass on th heritage of spiritual Messianic Jewish life. Softcover, 86 pages

978-1936716739 **LB93** $8.99

That They May Be One *A Brief Review of Church Restoration Movements and Their Connection to the Jewish People*

—Daniel Juster, Th.D

Something prophetic and momentous is happening. The Church is finally fully grasping its relationship to Israel and the Jewish people. Author describes the restoration movements in Church history and how they connected to Israel and the Jewish people. Each one contributed in some way—some more, some less—toward the ultimate unity between Jews and Gentiles. Predicted in the Old Testament and fulfilled in the New, Juster believes this plan of God finds its full expression in Messianic Judaism. He may be right. See what you think as you read *That They May Be One*. 100 pages.

978-1880226711 **LB71** $9.99

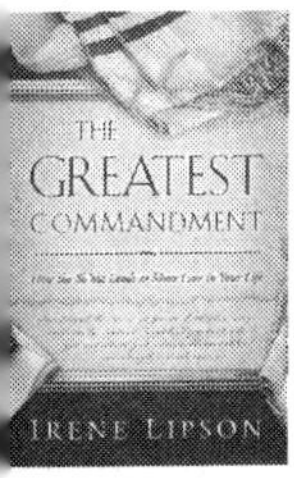

The Greatest Commandment

How the Sh'ma Leads to More Love in Your Life

—Irene Lipson

"What is the greatest commandment?" Yeshua was asked. His reply—"Hear, O Israel, the Lord our God, the Lord is one, and you are to love Adonai your God with all your heart, with all your soul, with all your understanding, and all your strength." A superb book explaining each word so the meaning can be fully grasped and lived. Endorsed by Elliot Klayman, Susan Perlman, & Robert Stearns. 175 pages.

978-1880226360 **LB65** $12.99

Blessing the King of the Universe

Transforming Your Life Through the Practice of Biblical Praise

—Irene Lipson

Insights into the ancient biblical practice of blessing God are offered clearly and practically. With examples from Scripture and Jewish tradition, this book teaches the biblical formula used by men and women of the Bible, including the Messiah; points to new ways and reasons to praise the Lord; and explains more about the Jewish roots of the faith. Endorsed by Rabbi Barney Kasdan, Dr. Mitch Glaser, & Rabbi Dr. Dan Cohn-Sherbok. 144 pages.

978-1880226797 **LB53** $11.99

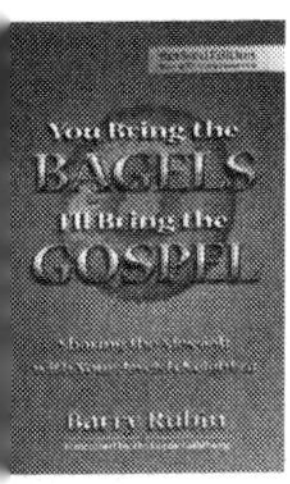

You Bring the Bagels, I'll Bring the Gospel

Sharing the Messiah with Your Jewish Neighbor

Revised Edition—Now with Study Questions

—Rabbi Barry Rubin

This "how-to-witness-to-Jewish-people" book is an orderly presentation of everything you need to share the Messiah with a Jewish friend. Includes Messianic prophecies, Jewish objections to believing, sensitivities in your witness, words to avoid. A "must read" for all who care about the Jewish people. Good for individual or group study. Used in Bible schools. Endorsed by Harold A. Sevener, Dr. Walter C. Kaiser, Dr. Erwin J. Kolb and Dr. Arthur F. Glasser. 253 pages.

English	978-1880226650	**LB13**	$12.99
Te Tengo Buenas Noticias	978-0829724103	**OBSP02**	$14.99

Making Eye Contact With God

A Weekly Devotional for Women

—Terri Gillespie

What kind of eyes do you have? Are they downcast and sad? Are they ful of God's joy and passion? See yourself through the eyes of God. Using rea life anecdotes, combined with scripture, the author reveals God's heart fo women everywhere, as she softly speaks of the ways in which women se God. Endorsed by prominent authors: Dr. Angela Hunt, Wanda Dyson an Kathryn Mackel. 247 pages, hardcover.

978-1880226513 **LB68** $19.99

Divine Reversal

The Transforming Ethics of Jesus

—Rabbi Russell Resnik

In the Old Testament, God often reversed the plans of man. Yeshua' ethics continue this theme. Following his path transforms one's life fron within, revealing the source of true happiness, forgiveness, reconciliatior fidelity and love. From the introduction, "As a Jewish teacher, Jesus doesn' separate matters of theology from practice. His teaching is consistentl practical, ethical, and applicable to real life, even two thousand years afte it was originally given." Endorsed by Jonathan Bernis, Dr. Daniel C. Juste Dr. Jeffrey L. Seif, and Dr Darrell Bock. 206 pages

978-1880226803 **LB72** $12.99

Praying Like the Jew, Jesus

Recovering the Ancient Roots of New Testament Prayer

—Dr. Timothy P. Jones

This eye-opening book reveals the Jewish background of many of Yeshua' prayers. Historical vignettes "transport" you to the times of Yeshua s you can grasp the full meaning of Messiah's prayers. Unique devotiona thoughts and meditations, presented in down-to-earth language, provid inspiration for a more meaningful prayer life and help you draw closer t God. Endorsed by Mark Galli, James W. Goll, Rev. Robert Stearns, Jame F. Strange, and Dr. John Fischer. 144 pages.

978-1880226285 **LB56** $9.99

Growing Your Olive Tree Marriage *A Guide for Couple from Two Traditions*

—David J. Rudolph

One partner is Jewish; the other is Christian. Do they celebrate Hanukkah Christmas or both? Do they worship in a church or a synagogue? How wi the children be raised? This is the first book from a biblical perspective tha addresses the concerns of intermarried couples, offering a godly solutior Includes highlights of interviews with intermarried couples. Endorse by Walter C. Kaiser, Jr., Rabbi Dan Cohn-Sherbok, Jonathan Settel, D Mitchell Glaser & Natalie Sirota. 224 pages.

978-1880226179 **LB50** $12.99

In Search of the Silver Lining *Where is God in the Midst of Life's Storms?*

—Jerry Gramckow

When faced with suffering, what are your choices? Storms have always raged. And people have either perished in their wake or risen above the tempests, shaping history by their responses…new storms are on the horizon. How will we deal with them? How will we shape history or those who follow us? The answer lies in how we view God in the midst of the storms. Endorsed by Joseph C. Aldrich, Ray Beeson, Dr. Daniel Juster. 176 pages.

978-1880226865 **LB39** $10.99

The Voice of the Lord *Messianic Jewish Daily Devotional*

—Edited by David J. Rudolph

Brings insight into the Jewish Scriptures—both Old and New Testaments. Twenty-two prominent Messianic contributors provide practical ways to apply biblical truth. Start your day with this unique resource. Explanatory notes. Perfect companion to the Complete Jewish Bible (see page 2). Endorsed by Edith Schaeffer, Dr. Arthur F. Glaser, Dr. Michael L. Brown, Mitch Glaser and Moishe Rosen. 416 pages.

9781880226704 **LB31** $19.99

Kingdom Relationships *God's Laws for the Community of Faith*

—Dr. Ron Moseley

Dr. Ron Moseley's Yeshua: A Guide to the Real Jesus and the Original Church has taught thousands of people about the Jewishness of not only Yeshua, but of the first followers of the Messiah.

In this work, Moseley focuses on the teaching of Torah -- the Five Books of Moses -- tapping into truths that greatly help modern-day members of the community of faith. 64 pages.

978-1880226841 **LB37** $8.99

Mutual Blessing *Discovering the Ultimate Destiny of Creation*

—Daniel C. Juster

To truly love as God loves is to see the wonder and richness of the distinct differences in all of creation and his natural order of interdependence. This is the way to mutual blessing and the discovery of the ultimate destiny of creation. Learn how to become enriched and blessed as you enrich and bless others and all that is around you! Softcover, 135 pages.

978-1936716746 **LB94** $9.99

Train Up A Child *Successful Parenting For The Next Generation*

—Dr. Daniel L. Switzer

The author, former principal of Ets Chaiyim Messianic Jewish Day School, and father of four, combines solid biblical teaching with Jewish sources on child raising, focusing on the biblical holy days, giving fresh insight into fulfilling the role of parent. 188 pages. Endorsed by Dr. David J. Rudolph, Paul Lieberman, and Dr. David H. Stern.

978-1880226377 **LB64** $12.99

Fire on the Mountain - *Past Renewals, Present Revivals and the Coming Return of Israel*

—Dr. Louis Goldberg

The term "revival" is often used to describe a person or congregatio turning to God. Is this something that "just happens," or can it be brough about? Dr. Louis Goldberg, author and former professor of Hebrew an Jewish Studies at Moody Bible Institute, examines real revivals that too place in Bible times and applies them to today. 268 pages.

978-1880226858 **LB38** $15.99

Voices of Messianic Judaism *Confronting Critical Issues Facing a Maturing Movement*

—General Editor Rabbi Dan Cohn-Sherbok

Many of the best minds of the Messianic Jewish movement contribute their thoughts to this collection of 29 substantive articles. Challengin questions are debated: The involvement of Gentiles in Messianic Judaism How should outreach be accomplished? Liturgy or not? Intermarriage 256 pages.

978-1880226933 **LB46** $15.99

The Enduring Paradox *Exploratory Essays in Messianic Judaism*

—General Editor Dr. John Fischer

Yeshua and his Jewish followers began a new movement—Messiani Judaism—2,000 years ago. In the 20th century, it was reborn. Now, a the beginning of the 21st century, it is maturing. Twelve essays from to contributors to the theology of this vital movement of God, including: D Walter C. Kaiser, Dr. David H. Stern, and Dr. John Fischer. 196 pages.

978-1880226902 **LB43** $13.99

The World To Come *A Portal to Heaven on Earth*

—Derek Leman

An insightful book, exposing fallacies and false teachings surrounding thi extremely important subject... paints a hopeful picture of the future an dispels many non-biblical notions. Intriguing chapters: Magic and Desire The Vision of the Prophets, Hints of Heaven, Horrors of Hell, The Drama o the Coming Ages. Offers a fresh, but old, perspective on the world to come as it interacts with the prophets of Israel and the Bible. 110 pages.

978-1880226049 **LB67** .$9.9

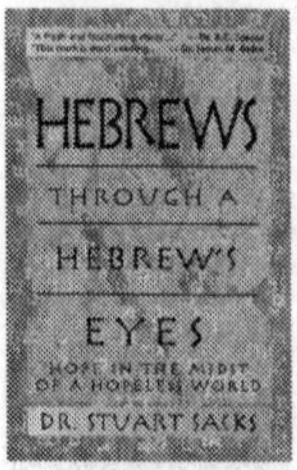

Hebrews Through a Hebrew's Eyes

—Dr. Stuart Sacks

Written to first-century Messianic Jews, this epistle, understood throug Jewish eyes, edifies and encourages all. 119 pages. Endorsed by Dr. R.C Sproul and James M. Boice.

978-1880226612 **LB23** $10.99

The Irrevocable Calling *Israel's Role As A Light To The Nations*

—Daniel C. Juster, Th.D.

Referring to the chosen-ness of the Jewish people, Paul, the Apostle, wrote "For God's free gifts and his calling are irrevocable" (Rom. 11:29). This messenger to the Gentiles understood the unique calling of his people, Israel. So does Dr. Daniel Juster, President of Tikkun Ministries Int'l. In *The Irrevocable Calling*, he expands Paul's words, showing how Israel was uniquely chosen to bless the world and how these blessings can be enjoyed today. Endorsed by Dr. Jack Hayford, Mike Bickle and Don Finto. 64 pages.

978-1880226346 **LB66** $8.99

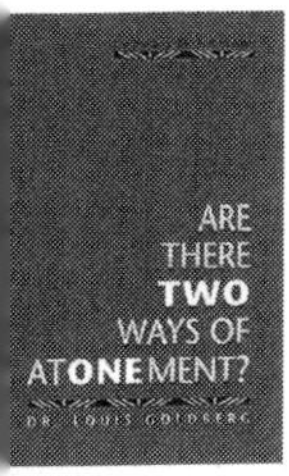

Are There Two Ways of Atonement?

—Dr. Louis Goldberg

Here Dr. Louis Goldberg, long-time professor of Jewish Studies at Moody Bible Institute, exposes the dangerous doctrine of Two-Covenant Theology. 32 pages.

978-1880226056 **LB12** $ 4.99

Awakening *Articles and Stories About Jews and Yeshua*

—Arranged by Anna Portnov

Articles, testimonies, and stories about Jewish people and their relationship with God, Israel, and the Messiah. Includes the effective tract, "The Most Famous Jew of All." One of our best anthologies for witnessing to Jewish people. Let this book witness for you! Russian version also available. 110 pages.

English	978-1880226094	**LB15**	$ 6.99
Russian	978-1880226018	**LB14**	$ 6.99

The Unpromised Land *The Struggle of Messianic Jews Gary and Shirley Beresford*

—Linda Alexander

They felt God calling them to live in Israel, the Promised Land. Wanting nothing more than to live quietly and grow old together in the country of refuge for all Jewish people, little did they suspect what events would follow to try their faith. The fight to make *aliyah*, to claim their rightful inheritance in the Promised Land, became a battle waged not only for themselves, but also for Messianic Jews all over the world that wish to return to the Jewish homeland. Here is the true saga of the Beresford`s journey to the land of their forefathers. 216 pages.

978-1880226568 **LB19** $ 9.99

Death of Messiah *Twenty fascinating articles that address a subject of grief, hope, and ultimate triumph.*
—Edited by Kai Kjaer-Hansen

This compilation, written by well-known Jewish believers, addresses the issue of Messiah and offers proof that Yeshua—the true Messiah—not only died, but also was resurrected! 160 pages.

978-1880226582 **LB20** $ 8.99

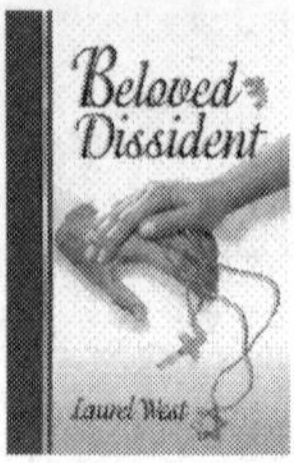

Beloved Dissident *(A Novel)*
—Laurel West

A gripping story of human relationships, passionate love, faith, and spiritual testing. Set in the world of high finance, intrigue, and international terrorism, the lives of David, Jonathan, and Leah intermingle on many levels--especially their relationships with one another and with God. As the two men tangle with each other in a rising whirlwind of excitement and danger, each hopes to win the fight for Leah's love. One of these rivals will move Leah to a level of commitment and love she has never imagined--or dared to dream. Whom will she choose? 256 pages.

978-1880226766 **LB33** $ 9.99

Sudden Terror
—Dr. David Friedman

Exposes the hidden agenda of militant Islam. The author, a former member of the Israel Defense Forces, provides eye-opening information needed in today's dangerous world.
Dr. David Friedman recounts his experiences confronting terrorism; analyzes the biblical roots of the conflict between Israel and Islam; provides an overview of early Islam; demonstrates how the United States and Israel are bound together by a common enemy; and shows how to cope with terrorism and conquer fear. The culmination of many years of research and personal experiences. This expose will prepare you for what's to come! 160 pages.

978-1880226155 **LB49** $ 9.99

It is Good! *Growing Up in a Messianic Family*
—Steffi Rubin

Growing up in a Messianic Jewish family. Meet Tovah! Tovah (Hebrew for "Good") is growing up in a Messianic Jewish home learning the meaning of God`s special days. Ideal for young children, it teaches the biblical holidays and celebrates faith in Yeshua. 32 pages to read & color.

978-1880226063 **LB11** $ 4.99
